AI AND ITS TRAJECTORY:
Navigating the Age of Enlightenment and Addressing the Threats to Humanity

Our future rests in our hands. By creating cultures of ethical innovation, inclusion and collaboration, we can ensure that AI is a social medicine that heals, not a poison that sickens. This will require the concerted work of technologists, policymakers, educators and the public to ensure that the future of AI is one that promotes human flourishing and social good.

This demonstrates the necessity of this book for everyone who wants to both understand, and participate in, the dramatic shift AI may yet make happen for humanity. It is a call, and an invitation, to act and engage – for the better.

We hope "AI and Its Trajectory: Navigating the Age of Enlightenment and Overcoming the Threats to Humanity" inspires you to the possibilities of AI and gives you the insights and understanding to shape the destiny and future of AI so that we can ensure its benefits to all of humanity.

DR. Selva Sugunendran

CEng, MIEE, MCMI, CHt, MIMDHA, MBBNLP, MGO¬NLP, DBS
AI Robotics Strategist & Visionary Author,
1 Best Selling Author, Speaker & Coach
Website: Https://AIRoboticsForGood.com
Email: Selva@AIRoboticsForGood.com

Medical Disclaimer: The author of this book is a competent, experienced writer. He has taken every opportunity to ensure that all information presented here is correct and up to date at the time of writing. No documentation within this book has been evaluated by the Food and Drug Administration, and no documentation should be used to diagnose, treat, cure, or prevent any disease.

Any information is to be used for educational and information purposes only. It should never be substituted for the medical advice from your doctor or other health care professionals.

We do not dispense medical advice, prescribe drugs, or diagnose any illnesses with our literature.

The author and publisher are not responsible or liable for any self or third-party diagnosis made by visitors based upon the content of this book. The author or publisher does not in any way endorse any commercial products or services linked from other websites to this book.

Please, always consult your doctor or health care specialist if you are in any way concerned about your physical wellbeing.

Contents

About The Author

DR SELVA SUGUNENDRAN has performed many lofty positions in life, the most uplifting to him is the one he chose, which was to serve mankind by showing them the way to health, wealth, and success.

Upon selling his UK based Integrated High Security IT company which he ran for 25 years as the company owner, he took the "jump" out of the corporate world into his passion for helping people to be more, do more and get more out of their life than they ever thought possible! Young or old, he helped them create a new blueprint for life that literally changed their world and continues to do so.

As a result of that work, he was attracted to study, research, write and publish 50+ books of which 6 books were #1 Best Sellers in genres Health & Wellness, Alzheimer's / Dementia, Success in Business &Life, and Christianity & more recently on AI & Robotics

He has developed a special Ai- Robotic Machine (which is currently in a prototype stage) which can be used as a "Virtual Carer" for Dementia patients who live alone and cannot afford 24-hour care.

He has published several books on AI Robotics. These include the following: "AI For Beginners", "Rogue AI-The Oppenheimer Effect", "Mastering the minds of machines", "AI Trilogy, AI Game Changers", "AI and its Trajectory "and "Superhumans vs Humans-Embracing the next frontier."

Foreword

This foreword sets the stage for a thoughtful and comprehensive exploration of AI, inviting readers to understand and engage with both its potential and its challenges.

I feel very privileged to be invited to write the Foreword to this masterpiece by DR. Selva, who is well known as an AI and Robotics Strategist and Visionary Author.

As we stand on the precipice of unprecedented technological advancement, the emergence of artificial intelligence (AI) heralds both tremendous opportunities and formidable challenges. "AI and Its Trajectory: Navigating the Age of Enlightenment and Addressing the Threats to Humanity" by DR Selva embarks on an in-depth exploration of this duality, providing a comprehensive guide to understanding and harnessing the power of AI responsibly.

A New Age of Enlightenment

AI represents a new era of enlightenment, analogous to the scientific and philosophical advancements of the 18th century. This modern enlightenment is characterized by the unparalleled capability of AI systems to process and analyse vast amounts of data, leading to breakthroughs in numerous fields including healthcare, climate science, and more. AI's potential to solve complex problems and generate new knowledge mirrors the transformative impact of the Enlightenment, promising profound improvements in our quality of life.

Balancing Innovation with Ethical Responsibility

As DR. Selva says, "With the transformative power of AI comes a significant ethical responsibility". The book addresses critical concerns such as bias in AI algorithms, privacy, accountability, and the ethical implications of autonomous systems. As AI systems are only as unbiased as the data they are trained on, ensuring fairness and transparency in AI development is paramount. The ethical deployment of AI in areas such as law enforcement, finance, and healthcare are crucial to maintaining public trust and preventing the exacerbation of social inequalities.

Preparing for an AI-Driven Future

As AI continues to evolve, so too must our approach to education and workforce development. The book emphasizes the need for lifelong learning and the continuous adaptation of skills to keep pace with technological advancements. It highlights the importance of preparing individuals for new roles that combine traditional expertise with AI competencies, ensuring that workers are equipped to thrive in an AI-driven economy.

Promoting Social Equity and Bridging the Digital Divide

One of AI's most promising potentials lies in its ability to promote social equity. However, this potential can only be realized if we address the digital divide and ensure equitable access to AI technologies. By providing underserved communities with the necessary resources and support, we can leverage AI for economic and social advancement. Additionally, fostering diversity and inclusion in AI development is critical to creating technologies that serve the needs of all societal segments.

AI and Environmental Sustainability

The book also delves into the role of AI in promoting environmental sustainability. AI technologies can optimize energy usage, predict climate change impacts, and manage natural resources more effectively. By leveraging AI, we can develop innovative solutions to mitigate climate change and ensure a sustainable future for generations to come.

Human Creativity and AI

AI is not just a tool for efficiency; it also serves as a catalyst for creativity. In the arts, AI is pushing the boundaries of what is possible, from composing music to creating visual art. This intersection of AI and human creativity opens new frontiers for artistic expression, though it also raises questions about authorship and the nature of creativity itself.

Navigating the AI Revolution

As we navigate the AI revolution, it is essential to balance the opportunities with the challenges. This book provides a roadmap for understanding AI's trajectory, highlighting both the promises and the risks. Through comprehensive analysis and real-world examples, it explores how AI is transforming various sectors and examines the ethical, social, and economic implications of this transformative technology.

A Call to Action

The future of AI is in our hands. By fostering a culture of ethical innovation, inclusivity, and collaboration, we can ensure that AI serves as a force for good in our society. This book is a call to action for all those wishing to engage with the transformative power of AI. It invites readers to explore the possibilities, confront the challenges, and contribute to shaping a future where AI benefits all of humanity.

As you embark on this journey through the pages of "AI and Its Trajectory: Navigating the Age of Enlightenment and Addressing the Threats to Humanity," we hope to inspire you with the potential of AI and equip you with the knowledge and insights needed to navigate the complex landscape of this revolutionary technology. Together, we can chart a course toward a future where AI serves as a beacon of progress, equity, and sustainability.

Matt Morrison

Introduction:
The Transformative Power of AI

The future is no longer artificial intelligence. It is here, with us. The technologies of artificial intelligence permeate every aspect of our work and daily life – how we interact, think and play. Ever-improving artificial intelligence (AI) technologies are solving problems at an unprecedented speed and scale, increasing efficiencies, and extending human capabilities. However, harnessing AI's potential for positive effects requires us to confront some uncomfortable ethical, social and economic challenges. The question is not whether we can overcome the challenges inherent in this endeavour. The challenges are real; the consequences are profound.

Through a holistic landscape analysis in this volume, AI and Its Trajectory: the Age of Enlightenment and the Threats to Humanity (Acumen), this book considers the wide consequences of artificial intelligence, as well as to examine the promises and pitfalls of this emerging technology. It analyses how artificial intelligence is impacting different lines of work as well as what we should do to secure its future wisely and ethically.

The Dawn of AI: An Age of Enlightenment

For the first time in our history, the rise of AI represents the thrust of truly new enlightened era – an information and data-driven enlightenment powered by intelligent algorithms. Just like the initial Enlightenment period that transformed our history with new explosive discoveries in science, philosophy and society, this is an entirely new emergent Enlightenment powered by AI.

At processing and analysing big data AI has outpaced us. Thus, thanks to AI we have made breakthroughs in medicine (for example, diagnosis of diseases is taken over by AI algorithms that can do this better than humans), climate science (weather and climate-change forecasting takes place thanks to AI models), to name a few. The AI age is the age of discoveries, and now we possess tools for solutions of the most important questions that we have been dealing with in recent years.

The Ethical Imperative: Balancing Innovation with Responsibility

With great power comes great responsibility. As we harness the potential of AI, we must also tackle its moral conundrums. AI systems can be as good as the data they're trained on, and those bulging data pools can hold biases out of which discriminatory treatment of AI users can easily emerge. The moral task lies in making them as fair, transparent and accountable as possible, to avoid AI compounding or intensifying social inequality.

Such systems can be deployed in critical areas such as law enforcement, the financial system and medicine. This gives rise to issues of privacy, consent and possible abuse, which in turn mean that developing appropriate regulatory and ethical guidelines is an ongoing challenge that everyone, from creators and users to the public at large, needs to grapple with. These ethical issues are discussed in detail in this book so that we can better understand the complex arena of AI ethics.

Preparing for the Future: Education and Skills in an AI-Driven World

Indeed, as the workforce becomes increasingly dominated by intelligent machines, the very nature of work is changing. Which sorts of jobs are going to disappear, and what new opportunities are coming into existence? To thrive as individuals in this new job market, we need to learn new skills and new ways to work, as education systems undergo radical changes to prepare individuals for the future. Instead of focusing on narrow technical skills, the focus should be on teaching young people to thrive in the turbulent world of work, learning skills such as how to think and be creative, how-to problem-solve and adapt to changing circumstances.

For this reason, lifelong learning and reskilling programmes for the existing workforce become important to help workers transition to new careers. The book then explores some of the emerging labour markets and new work arrangements, as well as workplace strategies for preparing the workforce for the opportunities and challenges of the AI era.

AI and Social Equity: Bridging the Digital Divide

It may be used to ameliorate social inequalities but, if not well-managed, it may widen the gap as well. It must, then, be accompanied by adequate investment, both public and private, aimed at ensuring that underserved communities and individuals are able to leverage AI technologies and bridge the digital divide. This also entails providing these communities and individuals with the opportunity and means to use AI for possible economic and social advancement.

Further, fostering diversity and inclusion – to ensure that AI reflects and serves the needs of everyone in society – remains crucial to building a robust and sustainable AI ecosystem. It is well-known that an inclusive AI economy helps create a world in which AI technologies benefit everyone, not just a global elite or corporations. This book offers a new perspective on how AI can complement social equity and socioeconomic lifestyles of marginalised groups. It concludes with recommendations for designing a new AI-driven world emphasising social inclusion and for building a more equitable future.

The Role of AI in Environmental Sustainability

Perhaps the most urgent issue of our generation is the quest to achieve environmental sustainability. Today, AI is leading the way with new solutions for addressing climate change, managing natural resources and promoting sustainability through every aspect of our lives. From optimising energy usage to ensuring the survival of plant and animal species, AI services are helping us steward the Earth.

The book reviews the contributions of AI to environmental sustainability, discussing how AI is used in the real world to combat ecological challenges, drawing on existing examples. AI has provided the tools to enable us to identify efficient solutions to relentless climate change and biodiversity decline.

The Intersection of AI and Human Creativity

Nor is it simply a useful efficiency-improver and problem-solver. Rather, AI is becoming a creator and innovator, particularly in the arts. Artists can use AI to create new musical compositions, visual works, literature and films. AI's processing power can analyse creative content on a macro and micro scale, revealing subtleties that can inform artistic composition. It can be used to spearhead artistic exploration that is yet to be conceived by a human eye.

But if people don't like the implications of these AI artworks for authenticity, for authorship, for originality, even for human creativity, this book documents the early developments in AI and the arts, showing both how the arts are changing through these emerging technologies, and what this might augur for the future of human expression.

Navigating the AI Revolution

The AI revolution is now upon us and will increasingly affect all of us in the decades to come. We believe – and hope – that this book will help people understand the path ahead. It won't be one straight road, full of optimism and gains without any regrets: there could well be detours ahead, awash with 'collateral damage'. Equally it could end up being a 'win-win' – humans coming to an accommodation with a world shaped by AI. The authors believe that it's still possible for that to happen.

We critically model AI's impact on domains such as health, education, governance, environment – and overall, while AI is providing personalised solutions and disrupting the social order everywhere, it brings with it a complex entanglement of ethical, social and economic consequences, especially as it also promises to solve the most pressing problems facing the world today. Against this backdrop, we present some ideas on how to wield it for a better world.

A Call to Action

Our future rests in our hands. By creating cultures of ethical innovation, inclusion and collaboration, we can ensure that AI is a social medicine that heals, not a poison that sickens. This will require the concerted work of technologists, policymakers, educators and the public to ensure that the future of AI is one that promotes human flourishing and social good.

This demonstrates the necessity of this book for everyone who wants to both understand, and participate in, the dramatic shift AI may yet make happen for humanity. It is a call, and an invitation, to act and engage – for the better.

We hope "AI and Its Trajectory: Navigating the Age of Enlightenment and Overcoming the Threats to Humanity" inspires you to the possibilities of AI and gives you the insights and understanding to shape the destiny and future of AI so that we can ensure its benefits to all of humanity.

DR. Selva

(AI Robotics Strategist & Visionary Author)

An important Notice

For those, who are totally new to AI and wish to learn more about AI, you could read DR. Selva's other books on AI, starting with **"AI for Beginners", "Mastering the Mind of Machines", "Rogue AI- The Oppenheimer Moment", "AI Trilogy" and "AI Game Changers: Revolutionizing Sports Training for Young Athletes"**

These books are all available on Amazon:

https://geni.us/betterlife

However, the current book can be read, understood and implemented without additional information.

CHAPTER 1

Introduction to AI and Its Trajectory

The Dawn of Artificial Intelligence

We no longer talk in terms of artificial intelligence (AI); now, we have artificial intelligence. The technology has emerged from the realm of science fiction to become one of the most important elements of modern technology, changing societies and economies across the world. From the voice assistant Siri to the machine learning algorithms that predict market trends: artificial intelligence is everywhere and all pervasive. In the following chapter, we give an overview of what AI is, where it originates from, how it is today and where it might be heading.

Origins of AI

The modern quest for AI commenced in the middle of the 20th century following the work of pioneers Alan Turing and John McCarthy. Turing is famous for his 1950 paper 'Computing Machinery and Intelligence', which contained a variation of the question 'Can machines think?' This marks the beginning of AI research. A year after Turing's paper, MIT computer scientist John McCarthy coined the term 'artificial intelligence' and in 1956 he convened the first workshop that has since been referred to as the 'birth of the field' of AI.

But early AI research was based on symbolic, rule-based approaches to reasoning and problem-solving, leading scholars to build programs for solving problems such as playing chess, proof of mathematical theorems and solving puzzles. Public enthusiasm was followed by harsh disillusionment when the limitations of early AI systems quickly became apparent, throwing the field into repeated periods of restrained funding, or 'AI winters.

Evolution of AI

New knowledge-based AI techniques called expert systems were re-kindled in the 1980s, which promised to solve specific problems in domains such as medicine and finance. But, weapons-grade AI intelligence really started with the development of machine learning (ml) in the late 1990s or early 2000s, when data and computation became available in large quantities.

A type of AI called machine learning (ML) represents a move to identify patterns and make decisions through specified rules. Instead of having to infer how to derive representations, the algorithm could be trained on data to come up with the rules itself. Pivotal ML improvements, especially in terms of deep learning (a type of ML that contains multiple layers of 'neural' networks) has accelerated this growth.

From natural-language processing (NLP) to computer vision and from robotics to autonomous systems, today we have AI applications that enable machines to comprehend and produce human language, familiarise themselves with objects and faces on images, drive cars, play complex games such as Go smarter than humans do, and perform many other tasks.

Current State of AI

Today's AI capabilities have increased an order of magnitude over the past few years due to advances in algorithmic methods, the availability of more data, and hardware performance. Several research areas and applications within AI include:

- **Natural Language Processing (NLP):** AI systems can both parse and generate human language. This area of AI operates the virtual assistants, chatbots and translation services we see around us. Technologies such as OpenAI's GPT-3 can write text indistinguishable from humans and hold human-sounding conversations.

- **Computer Vision:** AI can gain insight from imagery. Applications include facial recognition, self-driving cars, and medical imaging. AI-based systems can diagnose disease from medical scans with great accuracy. They can help health practitioners.

- **Robotics:** AI can help robots carry out jobs autonomously, from production and logistics to surgery and exploration. Meanwhile, robotic process automation (RPA) can complete mundane tasks in the workplace, such as in finance or customer service.

- **Predictive Analytics:** An AI algorithm aggregates historical data to predict future events; used in finance, marketing, health etc. AI can predict for example, stock market trends, customer behaviour and disease outbreaks.

- **Autonomous Systems:** Autonomous vehicles, drones and industrial machines are powered by AI, and are designed to operate with minimal human intervention: efficiency and safety stand to benefit.

Ethical and Societal Implications

As AI advances at an ever-accelerating pace, the question of what responsibilities we must address as ethicists to connect with and move along with these systems and technologies has increasing ethical and social consequences. These include everything from private information about ourselves to others, such as compromising photos or someone's diagnosis of a chronic health condition; patterns of racially biased treatment that we don't want others to model; the livelihoods of the millions of individuals who may be permanently displaced; and the proper maintenance of meaningful oversight mechanisms, effective mechanisms for redress, and a systematic approach to evaluation and scrutiny of the outcomes produced by such systems.

1. **Privacy:** AI systems will usually be reliant on large datasets including potentially sensitive personal information; thus data privacy and protections are vital to their being trusted.

2. **Bias:** AI systems can inherit bias implicit in the training data they use, leading to unfair overall results. Minimising bias in AI is crucial for fairness and equity.

3. **Job replacement:** Certain jobs can be displaced by automation and AI, particularly those that involve routine tasks. Reskilling and upskilling such workers for the jobs of the future is important.

4. **Accountability:** as AI systems make more decisions on their own, how are decisions made and who is held accountable for them? A set of guidelines and standards is needed to navigate this difficulty.

The Future Trajectory of AI

The future of AI will feature even more advancements and greater diffusion. I identify six key future trends and developments in AI. 6.2 Future Tendencies and Developments in Artificial Intelligence The future of AI will feature even more advancements and greater diffusion. I identify six key future trends and developments in artificial intelligence. 6.2.1 Future Tendencies in Artificial Intelligence. Today one can see the beginnings of the future developments in AI. There is a growing number of examples for the next stages of AI, including self-learning AI translate services like Google. It is safe to assume that similar advances in self-learning AI will be made in every field where there are adequate established linguistic rules, such as engineering, medicine, the law and many more. It is reasonable to expect that these next steps in AI will carry extreme consequences. One reason is that these steps in employing advanced mathematical applications, including in machine logic, will increase capabilities of AI to handle real-life situations where there is an abundance of rules and calculations, in fields where there are no adequate pre-established formulae – like in mathematics – but only experience, trial and error that generates data about correlations and causations. In these cases, an advanced algorithm can be a blessing. One may be that a next generation of AI, realizing its own superiority, may seek to rid the world of its omnipotent human inventor. There are realistic indications and arguments that AI already reaches a stage where new developments will have extreme implications.

- **General AI:** Current AIs are 'narrow' AIs, which are designed for a single task, but can only do that task very well (e.g., like AlphaGo or IBM's Watson). Developing general AI ('human-style' AIs) is a much longer-term goal. General AI would change a lot of things, but it also seems to pose very serious ethical and safety problems.

- **Human-AI Collaboration:** AI will complement rather than substitute human abilities. Collaborative AI systems will help professionals make better decisions, lead to greater productivity and innovation.

- **Explainable AI:** As AI systems get more sophisticated, it'll be important to understand how they make decisions. Explainable AI is designed to provide transparency and interpretation into AI's decision-making process, furthering its trustworthiness.

- **AI Governance:** Development of robust frameworks for AI governance, including ethics guidelines, regulations and standards, will be key to ensuring AI serves society's interests, while managing associated risks.

- **Social good:** As the world faces health, education, poverty and climate problems, AI will increasingly have a role in the struggle for a better social world. This requires driving AI across sectors and disciplines.

Conclusion

The development of AI technologies from the past to the present, and how this reflects the true nature of the journey is a remarkable achievement, with profound implications for humanity at large. Going forward it is important that we find ways to enhance AI technologies, harnessing this newfound tool for the betterment of humanity and society as a whole. The possibilities for artificial intelligence are truly endless and exciting, and their true future prosperity lies in how we navigate the path ahead, using this innovation in a sound and ethical way.

In other words, the ambition of the book is to provide, in full-length form, an integrated and authoritative account of the likely course of AI and its implications for the economy, for work, for the organisations in which we participate, and for society and politics. As we set out on that journey, chapter by chapter, we shall be scrutinising the forces and possibilities of AI, the contrasting threats and opportunities it poses, and the respective strengths and vulnerabilities of the strategies available to us in dealing with it.

CHAPTER 2

The Age of Enlightenment

Introduction to the AI Enlightenment

The age of reason in the 18th century, or the age of enlightenment, was a pivotal period in intellectual and cultural history. It refers to the movement towards a more secular and contemporary approach to society with rationalism, science and empiricism part of the fabric of an enlightened human condition. In similar fashion, we are currently witnessing a new age of enlightenment where artificial intelligence becomes the key, transforming our world, how we interact with it and augmenting human capabilities in an increasingly human-technology hybridised manner. In this chapter, key parallels between the historical enlightened age and the phenomenon of AI in contemporary times will be examined and explained.

The Historical Enlightenment: A Foundation for Modern AI

Intellectuals of the Enlightenment (the 17th and 18th centuries) helped provide the foundation of modern science and philosophy by questioning traditional authorities and urging people to seek understanding through human reason and empirical evidence. Pierre-Auguste Renoir (1890) Captured in the works of Immanuel Kant, Voltaire, Isaac Newton and others, the Enlightenment sought to answer age-old questions about God and the universe with empirical proofs. In this way, the Enlightenment provided a philosophical basis for modern civilisation, including individual liberty and truly unique human values such as progress, tolerance, human rights and liberty.

Key contributions of the Enlightenment include:

- **The scientific method:** With the rise of the scientific method

– systematic observation, experimentation and evidence-based reasoning – we entered a new era of growth and prosperity. This is the bedrock of much of modern science and innovation.

- **Empiricism:** An emphasis on empiricism (knowledge coming from the senses) helped to advance the new and eminently fruitful areas of physics, biology, astronomy and more.

- **Rationalism:** Rationalist thinkers claimed individuals can use reason and logic to discern what is true about the world and how to make the right choices. The focus on rationality undergirds AI research and development today.

AI as a Catalyst for Modern Enlightenment

The Enlightenment ideals are at the core of AI, which uses data, algorithms and computational power to further human knowledge and problem-solving capabilities. The AI revolution includes:

- **Data Scale:** AI systems sift through vast amounts of data, the data-driven approach parallel to the empiricism of the Enlightenment. Artificial intelligence now enables us to make evidence-backed decisions across all areas of life.

- **Automation of Reasoning:** AI algorithms can perform calculations and logical inferences at speeds never before possible. This constraint-free automation of cognitive tasks augments human capacities to overcome well-defined challenges that would otherwise remain unconquerable.

- **Interdisciplinary Collaboration:** The development of AI and its associated technologies requires interdisciplinary work between the sciences (especially computer science and mathematics, but also including neuroscience and the physical sciences, as well as engineering), the humanities and the social sciences, including ethics. The Enlightenment itself can serve as a model for these collaborative efforts.

Transformative Impact of AI

AI is creating transformative impact across most sectors of society, altering how we live, work and engage with the world.' The biggest changes are in the following areas:

1. **Medicine:** AI is moving a step forward in medicine with the ability to detect various health conditions earlier, to build personalised treatment plans, and to better allocate health system's resources. For example, new diagnostic tools powered by AI can review medical data to identify patterns and recommend further courses of action with high accuracy, as is the case with medical diagnostic tools released by IBM Watson Health.

2. **Education:** Online learning taught and developed by sophisticated personalised learning tools, such as Coursera, Udacity and Khan Academy. Students from all over the world are getting their basic education through these sites. They provide learning tools through suggested additional learning and self-evaluation for the students. The learning tools are regulated by artificial intelligence that traces the evolution of a student depending on the answers that he has entered. After evaluating the results, the tools of learning can measure the cognitive abilities of a student. If the tests show weaknesses or strong points, they make sessions that

facilitate and guarantee student's performance in a certain area.

3. **Finance:** AI is refining the world of finance by automating trading, preventing fraud and providing personalised financial advice. AI-based fintech solutions, such as robot-advisors, are also making financial advice cheaper and more widely available.

4. **Transport:** Autonomous vehicles and AI-assisted traffic management are changing transport for the better, making it safer, more efficient and environmentally friendly. AI-supported and highly automated transport solutions from companies such as Waymo or Tesla are increasingly available on the market leading the effort to build robotic cars that will reduce accidents and road congestion.

5. **Environmental sustainability:** AI can mitigate environmental challenges by improving energy usage, analysing climate trends, and aiding in conservation efforts. These systems can observe deforestation, track wildlife and ecosystems, and manage natural resources more efficiently.

Ethical and Societal Challenges

Alongside the incredible opportunities for transformation that AI promises, there are serious ethical and societal challenges that need to be overcome to ensure this is a positive transformation. Critical challenges include:

- **Bias and Fairness:** Accepting that AI systems can inherently reproduce bias inside their training data, accepting that the data used for training can be discriminatory, is one thing – but what we must not do is accept a discriminatory AI system with open arms. Avoiding bias requires rigorous testing of AI systems, making datasets as diverse as possible and policing (to borrow a phrase from Charles Bambach's book Living to Tell the Tale: A Daily Record of Life Beyond 90) to ensure the datasets are as bias-free as possible, too.

- **Privacy and Security:** As the personal data of millions is captured and analysed by AI systems, concerns around privacy and security are compounded. A strong framework of data protection and regulation is needed to protect consumers' rights.

- **Trust:** In ways not yet fully understood, the complexity of AI algorithms might make it difficult to understand how decisions are made. Consequently, the development of explainable AI systems that promote trust, accountability and transparency is key.

- **Loss of jobs:** A lot of jobs, such as those that involve routine tasks, could be replaced by machines. Training the workforce through reskilling and upskilling programmes would be important to mitigate the effects of job displacement.

The Future of AI-Driven Enlightenment

The future of the AI-driven enlightenment is characterized by several key trends and developments:

- **Human-AI Collaboration:** we believe that AI will enhance rather than replace human abilities. Collective AI systems will help professionals across a wide range of domains to be more accurate and efficient in their decision making, imagination and productivity.

- **General AI:** While existing AI systems are designed to perform specific tasks (or, as, in the case of neural networks, to perform a general class of tasks), it is important to distinguish general AI: systems that possess human-level general cognitive abilities. General AI represents the ultimate computer counterpart to the human intellect. Developing such a system would probably catalyse numerous fields and human endeavours, while also posing important ethical and safety questions.

- **Explainable AI:** With AI algorithms becoming ever more intricate, making black-box mechanisms clear has become an important goal, especially since it enables explanation and fosters trust.

- **AI 4 Good:** Practical application of AI for global problems including healthcare, education, poverty, food sustainability and the climate challenge can be undertaken and supported by coordinating AI activities across sectors and disciplines.

- **AI Governance:** Developing adequate frameworks for AI governance (including technical, ethical, legal and corporate standards and regulatory governance) will be crucial to ensure the positive impacts of AI for society while mitigating risks.

Conclusion

As the AI-powered Enlightenment leads to an era of previously unimaginable possibilities for extending human knowledge, efficiently solving problems and improving our quality of life, we recognise the unique role of this field in surpassing challenges of morality and society. With aspirations of combining the principles of the Enlightenment – reason, empiricism and collaboration – we hope that AI will lead to a better world.

My aim here is to convey that understanding, because AI will affect almost every industry, for better and for worse – but, ultimately, we have hope that we can use this fourth Advancement for the improvement of all humanity. If we can strike a careful balance between innovation and ethics, then we have a very good chance that this fourth Advancement will continue the upward arc of progress that humanity has experienced so far, bringing the best of benefits to our species and possibly to all life on our planet.

CHAPTER 3

Ethical AI: Principles and Practices

Introduction

As AI becomes part of every facet of human life, the question of how to develop and deploy AI ethically becomes even more pressing and important. In this chapter, we outline the key guidelines and various frameworks that undergird ethical AI development and application into human life. We look at the ethical questions that AI raises, discuss the role of regulatory frameworks, and identify the steps need to achieve ethical AI.

Understanding Ethical AI

Ethical AI is using technology to build and deploy AI in structures that reflect our collective, shared sense of what is morally right and good. And it is ensuring that AI systems are not unfair or discriminatory; that they are explainable and accessible; that they are designed responsibly, consider their impact on humans, and minimise harm. The aim is to derive the greatest societal benefit from AI and mitigate its most harmful outcomes.

Key Ethical Principles for AI

1. **Fairness and Non-Discrimination** - AI systems can and should be designed and trained to be unbiased and non-discriminatory. This means data for training AI systems should come from diverse and representative datasets; and techniques for detecting and minimising biases in AI models should be built into the systems. Fairness in outcome means that the AI's decision does not disproportionately adversely affect any individual or group.

2. **Transparency and Explainability** - AI systems need to increas-

ingly be explainable and understandable. All human users, as well as stakeholders, must know and understand how AI systems are leading to decisions, especially with regard to AI-induced directions and algorithms. Explanations need to be increasingly available on how models work and how the AI is trained, or how a particular algorithm is working. This is one of the more important emerging issues regarding AI in coming times: explainability is a key element as far as trust in AI is concerned, and trust is a prerequisite for any form of accountability.

3. **Accountability and Responsibility** - Developers, the organisations that deploy those systems, and the users of those systems must live with the fallout. There must be some recourse for complaints and redressing harm. Through the development of such institutions there needs to be greater clarity on lines of responsibility, so that responsibility – as more than mere lip-service to ethics – runs throughout the AI lifecycle.

4. **Privacy and Security** - AI systems must ensure the privacy of individuals. Strong frameworks for data protection must be implemented, data should be anonymised where feasible, and unauthorised access to AI systems and to the data these systems process must be avoided as far as possible. Privacy-preserving technologies should become the norm for AI development.

5. **Beneficence and non-maleficence** - Making good AI. AI should be good and do good. This includes not only an explicit requirement to avoid malicious behaviour (the ogle of the above diagram), but also ensuring that any AI application is 'aligned' with promoting human wellbeing and societal wellbeing. It is the re-

sponsibility of developers to think about the possible effects of such systems and implement defences against foreseeable harms.

Ethical Challenges in AI

- **Bias and Discrimination** - Since AI systems often repeat biases found in their training data, they can reproduce discriminatory outcomes in hiring, lending, criminal justice and other domains. Reducing bias is an ongoing challenge and will require continually working to increase the variety and representativeness of the data, in addition to improving methods for identifying and mitigating biases.

- **Lack of Transparency** Many current AI systems are also what's called 'black boxes', meaning that there's no serious attempt to explain how a system decides. This is a serious obstacle to holding the system accountable, and to trust in it. Finding ways to develop scientifically and technically credible AI models that we can explain is important.

- **Privacy Concerns** – Massive amounts of data are necessary to train AI systems, creating a heightened risk of violating people's privacy. Data protection standards and privacy-preserving AI techniques, such as federated learning and differential privacy, suggest ways of enforcing data privacy.

- **Security Risks** – AI can be vulnerable to myriad security problems, such as adversarial attacks (where attackers poison input data to fool the AI model) and essential monitoring and defence are required to safeguard these systems.

- **Autonomous Decision-Making** - It also concerns itself with questions such as how to ensure that autonomous AI systems, which will shortly be deployed in robotic cars and autonomous weapons, will make good decisions without human intervention. It is an important matter that needs to be addressed through 'mechanisms to promote ethical behaviour of autonomous systems.

The Role of Regulatory Bodies

Governments and regulatory agencies can also play a critical role in ensuring an ethical development and deployment of AI by setting standards and building guidelines and frameworks. This includes safeguards that align AI with societal values and lay out limits to ethical practice, whatever may follow. Regulations will not stop the spread of AI innovations but, by being flexible enough to account for the accelerated pace of AI today, they can provide clear ethical boundaries.

- **Establishing Ethical Frameworks** - Ethicists can offer frameworks for how AI should be regulated. These frameworks need to be developed through large-scale consultation processes among stakeholders such as industry, academia and civil society.

- **Enforcing Compliance** - Standards for what's considered 'ethical' need to be enforceable, with protocols for ensuring compliance. This means regular audits for AI systems, enforceable penalties and benefits for compliance with ethical AI.

- **Promoting Transparency** – Regulators can mandate transparency in AI development by making sure that enterprises disclose how their AI system functions, including what data is used, how it is processed and how decisions are made. Many researchers believe that transparency is an essential element in gaining public trust and in building accountability.

- **Supporting Research and Innovation** - Governments can invest in research into ethical AI but also support the development of tools and techniques that encourage ethical AI behaviour, such as the development of technologies that provide transparency, fairness or security.

Steps Towards Ethical AI

- **Integrating Ethics into AI Development** - Ethics should be integrated throughout the process of AI design, data collection, deployment and monitoring; they require an interdisciplinary dialogue between ethicists, engineers and other key actors.

- **Building Ethical AI Teams** – Organisations should form ethics-of-AI teams to oversee the ethics of an AI project, conduct ethical impact assessments, develop ethical policies, and assess regulatory compliance.

- **Engaging Stakeholders -** Ethical stakeholders are those who will be affected by decisions taken by AI systems – connect them with impacted communities and policymakers – and include a wide range of stakeholders.

- **Continuous Monitoring and Evaluation** - AI systems should be carefully monitored and measured to maintain ethical standards. This means regularly auditing their activities, incorporating feedback from their users, and responding flexibly to new findings or directions.

- **Education and Awareness** - Promoting education and awareness about ethical AI. By training AI developers and users in ethical principles and informing AI users – i.e., the public – about the benefits and risks of AI, progress can be made on ethical endeavours.

Case Studies of Ethical AI Implementation

1. **Healthcare AI** - Ethical AI is important in healthcare, for example in the diagnosis of diseases, so that patients are safe and have their privacy protected: systems must be trained on representative data sets so as to avoid biases; transparency is needed so that physicians can understand the AI's reasoning; monitoring the AI's output helps to make sure it is accurate and continues to be so.

2. **AI in Hiring -** AI hiring companies have the additional responsibility to test their software for bias and discrimination. This involves both periodic auditing and adjustments to the AI model until it passes certain thresholds when related to bias on the basis of gender, race or protected class. AI hiring companies have the additional responsibility to test their software for bias and discrimination. This involves both periodic auditing and adjustments to the AI model until it passes certain thresholds when related to bias on the basis of gender, race or protected class.

3. **Autonomous Vehicles -** The development of autonomous vehicles that are controlled by computer brains necessitates vastly greater ethical requirements, in terms of anticipating the correct

response in any number of possible scenarios related to safety, and especially on what to do in the rare situation when the AI is faced with a decision to destroy lives or prevent the destruction of human life. To ensure that an autonomous vehicle makes the 'right' decision should it hit something (as defined in a transparent and evident manner by those programming the vehicle), the computer brains would have to be extensively tested and the algorithms that drive that process made completely open and transparent – ensuring that life and human safety is given higher priority than property.

Conclusion

We need to develop ethics for AI, as well as create the necessary infrastructure that places the constructive use of AI – and consequences of its misuse – at the centre of a comprehensive approach. Through fairness, transparency, accountability, privacy and security, we can start creating AI systems that live by the values of their creators and the societies they affect. There is work to be done by regulatory bodies, organisations and individuals who can help steer the ethical AI we expect and demand. With continued monitoring and stakeholder engagement, coupled with education, we can walk the ethical tightrope of AI while also enjoying its benefits. As technological advancements gather speed, the need to remain ethically vigilant and proactive never looked more imperative than it does today, so we can ensure that humanity's future is built on the responsible pursuit of general AI, and the ethical use of its applications by those who can make the most of them.

CHAPTER 4

The Role of Regulation and Governance in AI Development

Introduction

With fast-paced AI development and its increased profusion in our lives, there is an increasing need for robust regulatory frameworks and governance models. This chapter looks at the importance of regulation and governance with regards to AI development, the currently existing frameworks and their challenges, and explores the way ahead to effective AI oversight.

The Importance of Regulation and Governance

Regulation and governance are crucial for several reasons:

- **Safety and Security:** In fields where AI systems will play an important role, like healthcare, transportation and financial services, it is important to ensure that they are safe and secure to the greatest extent possible so as to avoid harm.

- **Promoting equity and justice:** Regulations can be used to mitigate the tendency of AI systems to reflect, and even amplify, existing inequalities.

- **Earn Public Trust:** Transparency and accountability in governance will build public trust in the technologies, which is needed for acceptance and use.

- **Encouraging Innovation:** A clearly defined regulatory framework can create an environment of stability, enabling developers to understand the parameters within which they can operate.

Existing Regulatory Frameworks

Several countries and other bodies are now setting out frameworks for regulatory AI. Here are some leading examples:

- **The European Union's AI Act** – Leaders have looked to the EU, which proposed its AI Act last year: intended to govern all AI systems, the act categorises different AI applications as unacceptable, high-, limited- and minimal-risk. It requires all high-risk AI systems to be traceable, transparent, and have strict regulation and oversight.

- **The United States AI Initiatives** – in the US, the AI Initiative Act has been pushed to encourage RD while also outlining best practices for ethical AI deployment; and the US National Institute of Standards and Technology (NIST) has developed a framework for the management of AI risk.

- **China's AI Governance** - China has issued principles for the ethical use and governance of AI, stressing that AI should be 'controllable' and 'reliable', to be consistent with China's national security and social stability.

- **International Organizations** – the Organisation for Economic Co-operation and Development (OECD) and the United Nations have suggested norms and standards for nothing less than taking control of AI power, including principles for sovereignty, transparency, accountability and human-centric AI.

Challenges in AI Regulation

Despite these efforts, several challenges complicate the regulation of

AI:

- **Rapid Technological Advancements** - AI systems are constantly evolving and may well outpace regulation and regulators' ability to keep up with the rapidly changing technological realities, rendering regulation obsolete.

- **Global Disparities in Regulation** - It leads to a fractured global patchwork of different approaches in different countries, which makes life difficult for significant multinationals, and hampers developing global standards.

- **Balancing Innovation and Regulation** – It's one thing to want to encourage innovation and allow entrepreneurs to create amazing new things, but it's another to sit idly by while people get hurt or catch fire, no matter how tempting it might be to do so. Tilt the scales too far toward the former, and you risk becoming overly permissive when it comes to patents and market control. Tilt the scales too far toward the latter, and you risk under-regulation – what politicians sometimes refer to as 'deregulation' – which can result in abuse and/or harm. You don't want Uber to break down your front door just to take you to the airport. This type of technology moves fast, though, and the goal is to stay ahead of it, making it more available and allowing it to emerge in exciting and progressive ways.

- **Ethical and Legal Complexities** – Complex ethical and legal questions arise regarding liability when autonomous systems fail to perform properly. Dealing with such complex and multifaceted issues requires nuanced approaches.

Future Directions for AI Regulation and Governance

- **Adaptive and Dynamic Regulation** – set up agile and theoretically adaptive regulations: capable of evolving and becoming more sophisticated as technologies develop; that is, AI for the regulation of AI. This includes monitoring developments in AI and keeping regulations updated.

- **International Collaboration -** This will reinforce the useful element that many regulations provide (consistency and predictability for AI operations across countries) while hopefully mitigating the negative aspects that all legislation contains. International cooperation can also add some levers – such as international consensus or clear global standards – that can help move the needle.

- **Inclusive and Multistakeholder Approaches** - Diverse stakeholders (such as governments, industry, academia and civil society) should be part of deliberations about AI governance so that multiple constituencies have a voice, and regulations cover the full spectrum of interests.

- **Focus on Transparency and Accountability-** Requiring developers of AI systems to generate transparent documentation or explanation of how decisions are made in their algorithms.

- **Ethical AI by Design** - And third, embedding ethical values from the beginning of the process – into the design and ongoing training of machines – is much healthier than trying to patch bad behaviour on to mature systems afterwards. This means baking in 'ethical AI' at the start of the software lifecycle.

Case Studies in AI Governance

- **The GDPR and AI** - For instance, the EU recently enacted the General Data Protection Regulation (GDPR), a legal framework that has both broad societal impacts and implications for AI specifically, cantered on data privacy and protection. The GDPR's core principles of data minimisation, consent and the right to explanation are fundamental for AI systems that process personal data.

- **The UK's AI Strategy** - For one thing, the UK has a national AI strategy, one piece of which is designed to foster innovation and safety and a second for ethics. It has committed to funding for AI research as well as expanding the public sector use of AI, and formal AI ethics development work.

- **AI in Healthcare** - AI used for making diagnoses, developing treatment plans and a variety of other purposes in the health sector needs to be regulated, its designs monitored and tested for assuring patient safety and deployment appropriate for public healthcare and data protection needs. Examples from the epidemic fuelled applications of AI to healthcare can be found in different countries to this day. Interestingly, there is little transparency, oversight and addressable accountability of the AI designs claiming medical results that can endanger lives and introduce biased algorithms in vital public services. Case studies show the need for strict scrutiny and validation of AI systems used in healthcare applications such as diagnostics and treatment planning.

- **Autonomous Vehicles** – The deployment of autonomous vehicles appears to be rife with regulatory problems. Cases from the

US, Europe, and Asia reveal how they might ensure that robocars drive safely, reliably and ethically.

The Role of Ethics Committees and Boards

1. **Establishing Ethics Committees** – Businesses should set up ethics review boards to oversee developments and deployments of AI technologies and keep them accountable for ethical considerations. Such committees can provide consultations for ethical challenges, perform ethical impact assessment, as well as screen the process within the organisation to maintain ethical standards.

2. **Engagement and Transparency** – Since mistrust of AI is often tied to privacy breaches, democratising AI ethics and governance can help the public speak up about personal concerns. Transparency in AI's development and decision-making processes, for example, might help to allay people's worries.

3. **Ethical Training for AI Developers** - Developing ethical frameworks for developers that can be instilled in them through AI development training; for example, training around how to spot bias; how to handle data privacy; and how to make ethical AI decisions.

Conclusion

Significant regulation and governance will emerge to control the development and deployment of AI technologies, and if done in the right way it will make AI technologies into the great thing they can be, rather than a tool for a society that we want to avoid. We will need flexible, adaptive and dynamic regulation in the short term, alongside international cooperation, open and inclusive approaches, and prioritising transparency and accountability. By building ethics into AI through design and development, alongside more diverse approaches to engagement, we can create a world where all our AI technologies are safe, ethical and of benefit to everyone.

CHAPTER 5

AI and the Future of Employment

Introduction

From transport to manufacturing to customer services, every field of employment is being greatly influenced by artificial intelligence (AI) and its rapid development. This development leads to further changes in the employment landscape like the displacing of some jobs, the creation of new jobs, reskilling or upskilling the existing and new workers, and designing the future world of work in a balanced and inclusive manner. This chapter examines how AI transforms employment.

The Impact of AI on Job Displacement

1. **Automation of Routine Tasks** - Across industries, AI can automate many tasks that are routine and repetitive. In manufacturing, AI-powered robots can perform tasks such as assembly on the production line more accurately and efficiently than human workers. In services, AI chatbots and digital assistants can answer customer queries, thereby cutting down on the number of human agents who must deal with the same questions. As of the end of 2017, 42 per cent of companies had adopted AI technology, and the trend only accelerated in 2018 and 2019. Although automation increases productivity, it comes at the cost of workers: tasks that revolve around simple, repetitive processes are vulnerable to robotisation.

2. **Transformation of Middle-Skill Jobs** – Also, in the crosshairs of AI-driven automation are middle-skill jobs, which require at least some post-secondary education and training. Examples include administrative assistants, data entry clerks, certain technical positions and the like. Such jobs will call on workers to upgrade their skills.

3. **Sector-Specific Impacts** - Not all jobs will be affected by AI in the same way, either. In healthcare, AI can serve as a medical assistant, diagnosing patients and offering advice on healthy habits. In other industries, such as retail, we start to see more job losses as AI allows stores to operate with less cashiers and allows stores to manage inventory in more intelligent and effective way. Understanding these sectoral dynamics can be critical in helping strike the right approach and develop tools to deal with job loss.

Creation of New Job Roles

- **AI Development and Maintenance** – More AI engineers, data scientists, machine-learning specialists, AI ethicists and so on will be needed to build, maintain and tune AI systems. These professions will require high-level technical skills and knowledge of AI technologies.

- **Interdisciplinary Roles** - These cross-disciplinary roles reflect the fact that successful application of AI often requires integrating domain-specific knowledge with specialist AI expertise – for instance, in agriculture combining AI specialists with agronomists to adapt precision farming techniques, or in finance combining AI specialists with financial analysts to develop predictive models. Universities should welcome the emergence of the new disciplines required by these increasingly integrated practices.

- **AI-Augmented Professions** - AI can complement human skills, creating new job categories that use AI technologies. For example, in healthcare, clinicians aided by AI might allocate more time to understanding the patient and complex medical issues, while

AI manages routine diagnostics. Similarly, in education, AI could assist teachers to tailor learning for individual students, enabling educators to focus more on mentoring and creative teaching.

The Importance of Reskilling and Upskilling

- **Lifelong Learning** - As AI reshapes work, lifelong learning should be the norm. Labourers will need to supplement their training in order to remain relevant to the evolving job market. Government agencies, schools and employers will need to join forces to provide learners access to diverse, flexible learning opportunities that adapt to their needs and schedules.

- **Training Programs and Initiatives** – High-quality reskilling/upskilling programmes are vital for adapting workers to the AI world, e.g., through building not only technical capabilities (e.g., programming and data analysis), but also soft skills (e.g., problem-solving, creativity, empathy) and interpersonal skills (e.g., emotional intelligence). Examples of successes include organising closer ties between the business world and universities in the design of training programmes in line with labour-market needs.

- **Supporting Vulnerable Workers** - Special attention is required for more vulnerable workers exposed to different types of displacement risks, such as older workers, low-skill workers and people within racialised and marginalised groups. Targeted training and support can help them more efficiently acquire the skills and competencies to make a smooth transition and prevent the risk of economic fracturing.

Strategies for a Balanced and Inclusive Future of Work

1. **Policy Interventions -** Governments have the power to do so through their policies. Taxing firms who do not invest in reskilling their workers and subsidising companies that do, or regulating the labour market to reduce job polarisation, would all help create a more balanced labour market. Policies encouraging entrepreneurship and innovation could also support jobs in the innovation economy.

2. **Collaborative Ecosystems -** Collaborative ecosystems that weave together all the different constituencies cannot only spark new innovations and job creation; they can also provide the means to smooth and quickly disseminate the path to inclusion and ensure that the benefits of AI are widely shared. These ecosystems might include public and private-sector entities (e.g., public-private partnerships, industry consortia, governments at all levels, NGOs, firms and workers, education institutions, and community groups). They would offer opportunities for partnership and learning among these constituencies.

3. **Universal Basic Income (UBI) -** One of the solutions garnering support to ease the disruption that AI could cause to the economy is that of the Universal Basic Income (UBI). This strategy entails the offer to the entire populace of a basic financial allowance that would allow a worker, for example, the time not only to find education and training but also the possibility to become an entrepreneur or start any other activity they felt passionate about. Although the concept of UBI is controversial and disputed, there have been pilot programmes throughout the world that have yielded positive results in the sense that UBI has dimin-

ished poverty and paved the way for innovation.

4. **Fostering Innovation and Entrepreneurship** - Governments and private sector institutions can incentivise entrepreneurship and new business formation which in turn can help reduce unemployment and enhance economic development. Funding, resources and mentorship for startups and small businesses can help lower the entry barrier to entrepreneurship. AI technologies may further democratise entrepreneurship by facilitating the creation and scaling up of businesses, with comparatively low capital outlay.

Case Studies and Real-World Examples

- **Singapore's National AI Strategy** - Singapore took a broader approach, establishing a national AI strategy that encompasses the development of infrastructure, cultivation of research talent, promotion of AI adoption in industry, and training of the workforce for AI. This strategy includes platforms such as AI Singapore that provides grants and resources for AI research projects, to the Skills Future programme that provides training grants and learning materials for lifelong learning.

- **Germany's Industry 4.0 Initiative** - Through Germany's electrification programme (originally called Industry 4.0) its government has pushed forward both the digitisation and modernisation of the country's traditional manufacturing sectors through AI and automation. In the process, it has fostered cooperation between industry, government and academia to develop new technologies and provide training for the development of a new class of

skilled workers. Apprenticeship programmes and training courses are essential.

- **Microsoft's Global Skills Initiative** - Microsoft's Global Skills Initiative initially aims to help 25 million people across the world to gain digital skills, with an ultimate target of equipping 100 million people with 'research and development, engineering, data, AI' and leadership skills by 2025. Among the various course paths in a free skills programme run by Microsoft, ranging from 'AI' to 'data science' to 'digital marketing', the corporation teams up with non-profits, governments and educational institutions to 'democratise digital skills to empower economic opportunity'.

- **AI in Healthcare: The Role of AI in Medical Imaging** - In medicine, AI is transforming medical imaging by improving the speed and precision of diagnostic procedures. For example, algorithms can process medical images such as X-rays and MRIs, to detect unexpected findings, taking some of the burden from radiologists and improving patient outcomes. This case study nicely illustrates how AI can complement human expertise and explore new avenues for medical doctors.

Conclusion

In the long-term perspective of AI trends and the future of employment, there will be challenges, but also opportunities for stay-at-home moms to get a good-paying job like Diane did. AI-driven automation may lead to job displacement as many already have faced, but it will also create new jobs and improve on human abilities. This requires widespread reskilling and upskilling to ensure that the workers of the future have more opportunities for full and meaningful employment in the next AI-fuelled era. Governance institutions, educational institutions and private sector organisations need to work together to institute policies and other forms of activity to establish an equitable and inclusive future of work. The point is to stay innovative, ensure a social safety net for vulnerable workers, and ensure that AI's benefits bring benefits to all those who contribute to the phenomenon. AI technologies are no longer just a science-fiction fantasy, they are here today and will fundamentally transform employment and work. The future of employment is AI. Let's make it a better one.

CHAPTER 6

AI and Healthcare:
Revolutionizing Medicine

Artificial intelligence (AI) is poised to revolutionize healthcare, bringing transformative changes to diagnosis, treatment, patient care, and medical research. As AI technologies continue to advance, they promise to improve health outcomes, enhance efficiency, and make healthcare more accessible. This chapter explores the various ways AI is impacting the healthcare industry, highlighting key applications, benefits, challenges, and future directions.

AI in Diagnostics

- **Enhanced Diagnostic Accuracy** - AI algorithms, particularly those based on machine learning, have shown remarkable accuracy in diagnosing diseases. For example, AI systems can analyse medical images such as X-rays, MRIs, and CT scans to detect conditions like cancer, fractures, and brain tumours with a level of precision that rivals or exceeds human experts. These systems can identify patterns and anomalies that may be missed by the human eye, leading to earlier and more accurate diagnoses.

- **Predictive Analytics** - Predictive analytics powered by AI can identify individuals at risk of developing certain diseases based on their medical history, genetic information, and lifestyle factors. For instance, AI can analyse data from electronic health records (EHRs) to predict the likelihood of heart disease, diabetes, or stroke, enabling proactive interventions and personalized treatment plans.

- **Point-of-Care Diagnostics** - AI-powered diagnostic tools are increasingly being used at the point of care, such as in primary care settings or remote locations. These tools can provide rapid and accurate diagnoses without the need for specialized laboratory equipment, making healthcare more accessible to underserved populations. For example, AI-driven portable ultrasound devices can be used by non-experts to diagnose conditions in real-time.

AI in Treatment and Patient Care

1. **Medicine** - AI enables personalized medicine by analysing large datasets to identify the most effective treatments for individual patients. This approach considers genetic, environmental, and lifestyle factors, ensuring that treatments are tailored to the specific needs of each patient. For example, AI can help oncologists develop personalized cancer treatment plans by predicting how patients will respond to different therapies based on their genetic profiles.

2. **Robotic Surgery** - Robotic surgery systems, enhanced by AI, offer greater precision and control than traditional surgical methods. These systems can assist surgeons in performing complex procedures with minimal invasiveness, reducing the risk of complications and speeding up recovery times. AI-driven robots can also provide real-time feedback and guidance to surgeons, improving outcomes in delicate surgeries.

3. **Virtual Health Assistants** - Virtual health assistants powered by AI can provide patients with round-the-clock support, answering their questions, reminding them to take medications, and offering personalized health advice. These virtual assistants can monitor patients' health through wearable devices, detect early signs of health issues, and alert healthcare providers when intervention is

needed. This continuous monitoring and support can significantly improve patient outcomes and reduce the burden on healthcare systems.

AI in Medical Research

- **Accelerating Drug Discovery** - AI is transforming the drug discovery process by analysing vast amounts of data to identify potential drug candidates more quickly and accurately. Machine learning models can predict how different compounds will interact with biological targets, reducing the time and cost associated with traditional drug discovery methods. This acceleration in drug development can lead to faster availability of new treatments for various diseases.

- **Genomic Research** - AI is playing a crucial role in genomic research by analysing genetic data to uncover insights into the causes of diseases and potential treatments. AI algorithms can identify genetic mutations and their associations with specific conditions, enabling researchers to develop targeted therapies. For example, AI-driven analysis of genomic data has led to breakthroughs in understanding the genetic basis of rare diseases.

- **Clinical Trials Optimization** - AI can optimize clinical trials by identifying suitable participants, predicting outcomes, and monitoring patient responses in real-time. This leads to more efficient and effective trials, reducing the time required to bring new treatments to market. AI can also analyze data from previous trials to identify patterns and improve the design of future studies.

Benefits of AI in Healthcare

- **Improved Patient Outcomes** - AI's ability to provide accurate diagnoses, personalized treatments, and continuous monitoring leads to improved patient outcomes. Early detection of diseases and tailored treatment plans increase the chances of successful interventions and better health.

- **Enhanced Efficiency** - AI streamlines administrative tasks, such as scheduling appointments, managing medical records, and processing insurance claims. This allows healthcare providers to focus more on patient care and reduces operational costs.

- **Accessibility and Reach** - AI-powered tools can extend the reach of healthcare services to remote and underserved areas. Telemedicine platforms, supported by AI diagnostics, enable patients to receive quality care without the need to travel long distances.

- **Cost Reduction** - By improving efficiency and reducing the need for unnecessary tests and procedures, AI can help lower healthcare costs. Predictive analytics and preventive care can also reduce the financial burden associated with managing chronic diseases.

Challenges and Ethical Considerations

1. **Data Privacy and Security** - The use of AI in healthcare involves the collection and analysis of vast amounts of sensitive patient data. Ensuring the privacy and security of this data is paramount. Robust data protection measures and compliance with regulations such as the General Data Protection Regulation (GDPR) are essential to prevent breaches and maintain patient trust.

2. **Bias and Fairness** - AI systems can inherit biases present in their training data, leading to disparities in healthcare outcomes. It is crucial to develop and implement strategies to detect and mitigate biases in AI algorithms. Ensuring diverse and representative datasets and involving multidisciplinary teams in AI development can help address these challenges.

3. **Regulatory and Legal Issues** - The rapid pace of AI innovation in healthcare poses challenges for regulatory bodies tasked with ensuring the safety and efficacy of AI-driven medical devices and treatments. Clear regulatory frameworks and guidelines are needed to oversee the development and deployment of AI in healthcare.

4. **Ethical Use of AI** - Ethical considerations in the use of AI in healthcare include informed consent, transparency, and accountability. Patients should be informed about the use of AI in their care and have the right to understand how AI algorithms make decisions that affect their health. Healthcare providers must ensure that AI is used responsibly and that patients' autonomy and rights are respected.

Future Directions

- **Integration of AI with Other Technologies** - The integration of AI with other emerging technologies, such as the Internet of Things (IoT) and blockchain, can enhance healthcare delivery. IoT devices can provide real-time health data to AI systems, enabling more accurate monitoring and interventions. Blockchain can ensure the security and integrity of health data, facilitating secure data sharing and collaboration.

- **Collaborative AI Development** - Collaborative efforts between healthcare providers, technology companies, researchers, and policymakers are essential to drive the development of AI in healthcare. Public-private partnerships and interdisciplinary collaborations can accelerate innovation and ensure that AI technologies address real-world healthcare challenges.

- **AI Education and Training** - Educating healthcare professionals about AI and its applications is crucial for successful implementation. Training programs should be developed to equip medical practitioners with the knowledge and skills to effectively use AI tools in their practice. Additionally, AI developers should receive training on healthcare-specific requirements and ethical considerations.

- **Patient-Centric AI Solutions** - Developing AI solutions that prioritize patient needs and experiences is key to improving healthcare outcomes. Patient-centric AI tools should focus on enhancing patient engagement, providing personalized care, and supporting patient empowerment and self-management.

Conclusion

AI is revolutionizing healthcare by enhancing diagnostic accuracy, personalizing treatments, accelerating medical research, and improving patient care. While the benefits of AI in healthcare are immense, addressing challenges related to data privacy, bias, regulatory issues, and ethical considerations is essential to ensure its responsible use. By fostering collaboration, integrating AI with other technologies, and prioritizing patient-centric solutions, we can harness the full potential of AI to create a healthcare system that is more efficient, accessible, and effective. As we move forward, it is imperative to continue exploring and innovating in the field of AI in healthcare, striving for a future where AI technologies significantly contribute to the well-being of individuals and communities.

CHAPTER 7

AI and Education: Transforming Learning Experiences

Introduction

It would be difficult to overstate how swiftly artificial intelligence (AI) is changing how education happens. From ushering in an era of individualised learning to allowing for a near-complete retooling of administrative methodologies, the possibilities for how humans can interact and engage with educational material are limitless. This chapter identifies – and celebrates (mostly) – the multitude of ways in which AI is, is currently and will eventually, impact education; it outlines the myriad ways through which AI is being utilised, highlights its current benefits and potential pitfalls, and outlines the trajectory AI may be on from here on. By teasing out each of these aspects, we can draw a full and an ever-hopeful picture of how AI can aid us in creating a more effective, a more equitable, a more joyful educational landscape.

AI in Personalized Learning

- **Adaptive Learning Systems** – Adaptive learning systems use artificial intelligence to deliver education that is customised to each student's needs and pace of learning. Through data analytics, these systems analyse how well students are learning, and then dynamically adjust the curriculum accordingly so that students can progress more quickly. For example, Knew ton and Dream Box deliver unique math and reading lessons to students based on real-time assessment of their progress in mastering the content.

- **Intelligent Tutoring Systems** – Intelligent tutoring systems (ITS) emulate individualised tutoring by providing feedback and guidance based on a student's needs. AI can figure out where the student has struggled and make appropriate adjustments. The

AI-powered Carnegie Learning program, for example, provides individualised math instruction and practice in real time.

- **Learning Analytics** - Learning analytics serves to measure all the 'digital traces left by students' – that is, to collect and crunch data from student interactions, performance and engagement, using it to help identify at-risk students, glean insights into their progress, and adjust or enhance our teaching priorities and practices. Edmodo Insights helps teachers monitor, manage, and improve student performance; Blackboard Analytics does similarly.

AI in Administrative Efficiency

- **Automated Grading and Assessment** - The technology can help grading and assessment processes, saving precious time for educators; the systems can be also much more consistent than a single teacher. AI can easily take over multiple-choice tests and essays, but it is quickly advancing to even more complex assignments. Grades cope is one example of an AI application that can help grading written responses and give back detailed items of feedback.

- **Streamlined Administrative Tasks** - Administrative. It can and should be used to automate much of the department's back-office work, such as scheduling, attendance tracking, resource allocation, class scheduling, enrolment tracking, and utilisation of scarce resources. AI-powered systems such as PowerSchool and Brightspace can accomplish this easily.

- **Enhanced Student Support Services** – They can allow students to access immediate support and information from AI-driven chatbots and virtual assistants. Whether the question is about administrative processes or academic advice, a chatbot can supply the answer. Admit Hub and Ivy.ai are two chatbots employed by educational institutions to increase student services.

AI in Enhancing Educational Content

- **Content Creation and Curation -** via/this is an image of a virtually authored textbook; the prospect of this is both wonderful and worrisome AI could also assist with curation: issues such as the need for state-standards to be constantly updated, or subject-matter experts not spending the time to evaluate and select the best multimedia learning resources to incorporate into courses, could be addressed via AI. Content Technologies, Inc (CTI), for example, uses AI to create on-the-fly AI-generated (while guided by human education experts) textbooks and other learning objects.

- **Interactive Learning Experiences**, enabled by artificial intelligence virtual and augmented reality (VR and AR) content can fill a gap in learning styles, offering experience otherwise too costly or risky. VR, in particular, can recreate historical events, scientific experiments and complex problem-solving scenarios, giving the impression of first-hand experience. Google Expeditions and Space offer such applications that can be used in in a classroom.

- **Language Translation and Accessibility -** AI-powered translation tools can transform educational content, so it is accessible to learners with diverse linguistic needs and abilities. Real-time translation and transcription technologies help us overcome language obstacles and foster greater inclusion into our educational system. For example, Microsoft's Immersive Reader and Google Translate integrate AI technology to help support all types of learners.

Benefits of AI in Education

1. **Personalized Learning Experiences** – One of the biggest advantages of AI in education is that it will allow for the more detailed personalisation of the learning experiences students have. – If everyone learns new things in ways that suit their needs (problems and interests) and at the speed with which they can practise the information (e.g., one person likes videos and spaced repetition, another prefers books and active recall), it provides a better approach towards learning. – Not only are different people motivated to learn different material, but they also acquire and retain it in different ways.

2. **Enhanced Efficiency and Productivity** - AI can automate repetitive administrative activities freeing up educators from grading papers to better pursue their value-centred calling – teaching and enriching kids' educational experience through personalised instruction and meaningful, genuine interactions.

3. **Improved Learning Outcomes** - Through adaptive learning systems, intelligent tutoring and more, AI helps students learn better through tailored learning programmes, early warnings about who is falling behind, timely interventions, and data-driven insights about who is performing well and what additional supports would further hone their skills.

4. **Increased Accessibility** - AI provides translation tools for stu-

dents and academic articles in languages other than their own and supports students in learning through transcription and adaptive-learning tools.

Challenges and Ethical Considerations

- **Data Privacy and Security** – In AI education, student data will be collected and analysed at scale. The security of this data is paramount. Schools need to invest in robust data protection and ensure they are following regulations such as GDPR.

- **Bias and Fairness** - AI systems can reflect the same biases present in the historical data used to train them, harming students. We urgently need procedures to detect and remove biases so they're not embedded in the ways that AI algorithms operate. Diverse and representative datasets are key to fair AI.

- **Digital Divide** - Socioeconomic disparities can limit access to AI-fuelled educational material. Addressing the digital divide means efforts to ensure all pupils have access to the technology and connection to take advantage of AI-enhanced education.

- **Teacher Training and Adaptation** - While encouraging investment in educational artificial intelligence, it is important to ensure that teachers are able to adapt to new technologies and teaching best practices. Hence, appropriate training and professional development opportunities are key, to equip educators with the necessary tools to use artificial intelligence programmes in the classroom.

- **Ethical Use of AI** – Considerations of transparency, accountability and informed consent: students and parents need to understand the ways that AI is being used, and have some say into the kind of AI-driven decisions that are shaping their education. 2. Looking ahead: Principles for productive integration of AI Education has a crucial role in shaping the future of work, beauty, privacy, community and democracy. We are called on to collaboratively construct new principles that will guide the productive future integration of AI into those spheres.

Future Directions

- **AI-Enhanced Collaborative Learning** - AI can enable student collaboration in new ways by placing students in contact with other students, mentors and experts around the world. An AI-driven matching algorithm can be used to put students in contact with each other based on complementary skills and interests, encouraging students to help each other through peer support and peer learning. There are several collaborative tools such as Slack and Trello that could be adapted as educational tools to enable better collaboration and project-based learning.

- **Lifelong Learning and Professional Development** – AI will underwrite lifelong learning, helping everyone advance their careers. With personalised learning paths encouraged by AI, new skills and career progression can be actively pursued by individuals who want to stay current amid technological trends and job-market shifts.

- **Gamification and Engagement** – Incorporating gamification components with AI can help optimise students' engagement and motivation. AI can tailor the gaming learning experience, for instance, by customising the games based on different students' preferences in terms of the level of challenges and rewards. Kahoot! And Class craft are good examples of gamification in learning.

- **Emotional and Social Learning** - Emotional and social learning: AI feedback and intervention can help children transform their feelings into actions and connect with others. For example, AI can monitor a student's emotional state and adjust its interventions accordingly. Apps like Replica and Warbot can use AI to improve mental health and emotional wellbeing.

- **Integration with Emerging Technologies** – The same features apply even more strongly when we consider the additional potential of integrating AI with other emerging technologies, such as blockchain and the Internet of Things (IoT). We could see secure, transparent credentialing and certification using blockchain, and real-time monitoring and personalised learning environments using IoT devices.

Case Studies and Real-World Examples

- **Duolingo: AI in Language Learning** - One of the most common applications of AI is at Duolingo, an online language learning platform and mobile app with over 300 million users that functions like an AI-powered teacher scalable to millions. When you take the Italian test, your answers help shape the lessons Duolingo will prepare for the next person who takes the test, adapting the curriculum to their performance. Duolingo's AI turns language learning into an accessible and engaging experience on a mass scale.

- **Coursera: Personalized Online Learning** – Coursera uses AI to create personalised recommendations and learning paths for its users. It uses data about users to suggest courses that are related to their interests and goals.

- **Georgia State University: AI-Powered Student Success** - Pounce, the AI-powered system at Georgia State University, sends students personalised reminders, academic advice and early alerts if they are at risk of falling behind. The result? Significant gains in the number of students who make it to graduation and persist from year to year.

- **Squirrel AI: Intelligent Tutoring in China** - Squirrel AI, for instance, a Chinese company in the space of intelligent tutoring, is working with more than 20 million school students across China. It provides a customised education for each student by using an AI system that adapts lessons to the students' learning styles and paces, and offers tailored feedback and support. Squirrel has shown that student performance improves dramatically using their approach.

Conclusion

AI can pave the way through the development of personalised learning experiences, streamlined administrative capacities, and continuously improving educational content. The potential benefits of AI to learning are numerous, but generating and benefitting from AI will be contingent upon addressing challenges, such as addressing data privacy issues, assessing and tackling questions of bias, finding ways to address the digital divide, and helping educators adapt to more innovative classroom pedagogies. By working together to invest in teachers, ensure digital infrastructure is accessible, and embed ethical considerations into our practices, we can build upon current practices to maximise the potential of AI technologies in ways that improve education outcomes for all learners. The journey on AI in education is just beginning. In order to achieve a future in which AI technologies have significantly advanced learning and the lives of students across the world, we need continued exploration and innovation.

CHAPTER 8

AI in Governance: Shaping Policies for the Future

Introduction

Artificial intelligence (AI) is fast changing the way governance works, shaping policymaking, public administration and relationships between governments and citizens. Motivated by its transformative potential, governments around the world are integrating AI to make governance more efficient, improve public services and help policymakers make data-driven decisions. However, the growing use of AI in governance also raises serious concerns about ethical governance, data privacy and the need for accountable and transparent systems. This chapter explores the different ways in which AI is transforming governance, explaining its applications, its benefits, the challenges it poses and where it might go from here.

AI in Policymaking

- **Data-Driven Decision-Making** – AI enables evidence-based decision making sifting datasets looking for patterns and trends where humans cannot. Using AI, governments can inform policy decisions, model potential future outcomes and estimate what the result of different policies would likely be by analysing massive amounts of data. For instance, using AI the economic impact of fiscal policies could be predicted, or the environmental impact of changes to regulations.

- **Predictive Analytics for Policy Development** - With early warnings derived from predictive analytics generated by AI, governments could be equipped to more timely identify future, potentially transformative challenges and opportunities. With potential prescriptive options generated by machine-generated data analyses of what has worked in other places before, policymakers could be guided to respond more effectively to climate change, public-health crises like the Covid-19 pandemic or the Great Resignation, or structural fractures at the core of an economic system.

- **Optimizing Resource Allocation -** It can determine where resources need to be allocated and deployed to meet those demands – for example, by analysing healthcare utilisation data to ensure that the right people, beds and equipment are readily available to treat patients. Governments can use AI to distribute social services, infrastructure investments, and response efforts following natural and man-made disasters.

AI in Public Administration

- **Automating Administrative Processes** - AI tools can optimise time for activities that matter more for policymaking. Administrative tasks such as processing piles of documents, entering data and interacting with the public, can be automated, leading to higher efficiency, lower cost and fewer mistakes, freeing up employees to focus on more high-end, creative and strategic activities. For instance, automated chatbots can be used to field enquiries, process applications, and answer citizen questions in real time.

- **Improving Public Service Delivery** – There are many ways in which AI could facilitate these objectives. AI will offer better 'one to one' public service delivery experience for citizens. Just like AI chatbots offer tailored advice to bank or insurance clients, AI-empowered platforms can extract a lot of data about individual needs and taste of citizens towards a range of public services, e.g., bridge inequalities in public healthcare services, streamline specialised educational programmes to students' unique learning style or personalised delivery of tailored social services for those in need are among the ways that AI can facilitate better social equity and improve the overall public service experience for citizens.

- **Enhancing Transparency and Accountability** - AI could boost governance transparency and accountability through real-time data on government activities and effectiveness. AI-based data analytics can help shed light on all manner of government operations at federal, state or municipal levels – from spending on infrastructure or healthcare to streams of public revenue and payments. They can act as a more reliable check on the smooth and appropriate implementation of policies than audits or inspections. The wealth of accessible information may serve to maintain governments on the straight and narrow, as it could be shared in real time with all and sundry.

AI in Citizen Engagement

1. **Facilitating Public Participation** - AI can encourage public participation in policy governance by facilitating a channel for citizens to express their views, submit ideas and provide policy feedback. Sentiment analysis powered by AI can help to analyse public feedback and social media big data to measure public sentiments on a wide range of issues. Such engagement can help governments to gain insights into the needs and preferences of the public and make policymaking more advanced by incorpo-

rating citizen input.

2. **Enhancing Civic Education** - By personalising and engaging civic education, AI could contribute to the process of forming a citizenry with knowledge about civil rights and responsibilities as well as the workings of government and public policy. Therefore, AI could enable informed and active civic participation by expanding the number of citizens who demonstrate political knowledge.

3. **Predicting Social Trends** - AI can predict social trends. After digesting clean data from various social media, surveys and public records, it can provide governments with real-time insights into emerging issues. Governments can then quickly anticipate public sentiment, prepare for any potential challenges, and take pre-emptive actions to affect social change. They are well-positioned to pick up on cues that citizens' concerns differ from what is traditionally perceived.

Benefits of AI in Governance

- **Enhanced Efficiency and Cost Savings** – Robotics and artificial intelligence make governments more efficient, reduce transactions costs, optimise the use of resources, and improve the delivery of public services, thereby facilitating more effective use of tax revenue and allocating it to places where it is most needed.

- **Informed Decision-Making** - via AI-powered data and evidence, policymakers can objectively see what works and what doesn't, raising confidence and effectiveness of policymaking, thus enhancing the quality and effectiveness of a policy and its impact on the lives of society.

- **Improved Citizen Services** - As an example of how AI may improve public services, the paper points to the way that bots could use your call data record and location data to quickly let you know you might be eligible for public health support. 'Algorithms and artificial intelligence can give us one-on-one, tailored services that are efficient and can improve the citizen experience. The greater benefit could be greater trust in government because people recognise that it's focused on them, rather than adopting a "one size fits all" approach.'

- **Increased Transparency and Accountability** - By making government activities and performance publicly and transparently available in real time, AI will enhance confidence in government and hold public officials accountable for their actions.

Challenges and Ethical Considerations

1. **Data Privacy and Security** – The use of AI in governance will require collecting and analysing a huge amount of sensitive data. This data will need to be kept safe. Whenever is it stored in physical form or is accessible online, governments need to take precautions to prevent data breaches. Not only will they need to put in place analytics tools and other data protection systems to prevent external attacks, have to adhere to regulations, such as the European Union's General Data Protection Regulation (GDPR), to prevent any internal breach caused by careless misuse. This will be important if the government wants to earn citizens' trust.

2. **Bias and Fairness** - AI algorithms are more likely to inherit the

biases of the training data that they digest, making them more likely to deliver unfair outcomes when they are used to inform policy or provide a public service. There is an urgent need to develop and establish robust mechanisms to identify and mitigate AI biases. Diverse and representative data is essential for building fair AI systems.

3. **Ethical Use of A** – Transparency of use, accountability, and consent are key issues of ethics in the use of AI in governance. Citizens need to have information about when AI is used in governance, and there must be a right of the citizen to explain AI driven decisions relevant to their lives. Governments need to ensure that AI is used for good and in an ethical and proper manner.

4. **Digital Divide** – the digital divide threatens equal state provision of AI: if AI-enabled state services are not available to the entire population through access to appropriate technologies and digital literacy, then inequality could rapidly grow in the use of the governance of citizens through AI.

5. **Regulatory and Legal Issues** - The speed of AI innovation challenges regulators that are supposed to keep AI in check and guard against unethical and illegal applications of AI in governance. We need clear regulations and guidelines to better steer AI development.

Future Directions

- **Developing Robust Regulatory Frameworks** - Governments need to develop rigorous regulatory frameworks to assure the proper use of AI in governance. These frameworks should specify how to address data privacy and bias, assure transparency and accountability, but also allow for international harmonisation and best practices. International cooperation can be essential.

- **Promoting Transparency and Accountability** - AI-mediated governance can fail to live up to expectations and can sometimes produce perverse outcomes. Promote public confidence in AI-mediated governance by fostering transparency and accountability. Governments, for example, could improve trust by actively sharing information on how and why AI is used in decision making and public service delivery, and by investing in independent oversight boards with the power to monitor the technology and its use.

- **Investing in Digital Infrastructure and Literacy** – Making investments in digital infrastructure and digital literacy to equalise the playing field must begin with an economic plan that makes all citizens digitally literate, that allows for access to affordable internet and digital devices, and that enables not only equal access to but also spaces for agency in AI-driven public services.

- **Encouraging Public-Private Partnerships** - They can promote innovation and the general development of AI technologies that deliver public benefits. Finally, public-private partnerships can promote the development of AI systems responsibly by fostering collaboration among governments, technology firms, academia and civil society.

- **Fostering International Collaboration** – International collaboration to meet AI-related challenges and opportunities. There are cross-border governance dilemmas regarding AI. Here governments must work together to share best practices, develop international standards and figure out existing international cooperation for mitigating cross-border problems like data privacy and cybersecurity.

Case Studies and Real-World Examples

- **AI in Singapore's Smart Nation Initiative -** The island nation's Smart Nation initiative embodies this vision. Via AI software systems, it delivers public services more efficiently, improves urban planning, and empowers citizen engagement. There are AI-powered features for traffic management, public health monitoring and personalised government services via AI-sourced data from Singapore's public database. This shows that AI has a huge potential in making government more efficient and responsive.

- **AI in Estonia's Digital Government -** Estonia has been widely praised for its digitised public services, in large part due to its use of AI in several respects. The e-Residency programme, meant to maximise administrative processes and provide better, more personalised services to residents and businesses, employs AI chatbots and virtual assistants to facilitate citizen engagement and support public service delivery.

- **AI in the United Kingdom's National Health Service (NHS)** - For example, the UK's National Health Service is using AI to better deliver health care and allocate offers predictive analytics to assess patients' risk of developing chronic conditions and helps treat them appropriately and earlier. But AI is also used to battle bureaucracy and run the NHS more efficiently.

- **AI in Brazil's Public Security -** In Brazil, the government has deployed AI to boost public security by analysing data on crime, predicting criminal behaviour and optimising the deployment of police forces. The use of AI helps authorities detect patterns and tendencies in criminal behaviour and intervene before such activities occur, thereby helping to improve the public security in the country.

Conclusion

AI is facilitating governance by allowing for more data-informed decision making, the augmentation of public service deliverance and enhanced citizen engagement. Despite the beneficial contributions made so far, AI in governance still faces many challenges. The issues of data privacy, bias, ethical usage and the openness of the data divide must be tackled for greater public access. This requires robust regulatory guidelines, sorely lacking at present, transparent and accountable governance, inclusive investment in digital infrastructure and literacy, and public-private collaboration and international coordination. In doing so, we will not only gain the maximum benefits of AI for the public sector, but also realise a more efficient, responsive and inclusive form of governance worldwide. By continuing to research and innovate in AI in governance, we can create a future wherein AI technologies are strong contributors to the innovation and democratisation of public life.

CHAPTER 9

AI and Global Security:
Balancing Innovation and Risk

Introduction

Artificial intelligence (AI) is changing global security, opening up huge opportunities for countries to advance cross-cutting national defence, cybersecurity and law enforcement requirements and efficiencies. At the same time, AI also brings a number of risks such as the threat of misuse, ethical considerations and the necessity of a robust legal framework to regulate this field. This chapter discusses the dual-use nature of AI in global security by outlining its applications and benefits, outlining its challenges, and then assessing the strategies that will have to be put in place in order to balance innovation and risk.

AI in National Defence

- **Autonomous Weapons Systems -** Autonomous weapons systems – machines with artificial intelligence that can make decisions and engage targets on their own – are sometimes called 'killer robots'. These systems could increase accuracy, save human lives, and enhance efficiency. But would humans be held liable? And would these machines miss their targets? Shouldn't humans stay in control?

- **Intelligence Gathering and Analysis** – AI improves the fine-grained collection and processing of information from a wide range of sources (e.g., various sensors, such as satellite imagery, online social media feeds, or communication networks) to support enhanced target detection and pattern-recognition techniques based on machine learning algorithms. For example, national defence agencies can identify anomalies indicative of emerging security threats in unstructured surveillance video data.

- **Cyber Defence** – AI will be a cornerstone for cyber defence against threats and attacks, enabling AI-powered systems to detect and rapidly respond to cyber threats as they happen. AI can analyse applications looking for vulnerabilities and monitor network and device traffic to detect anomalies that could be a by-product of a cyberattack and take action to neutralise the threat – either by reversing suspicious modifications or shutting down the PC or network in real time to prevent data breaches. For example, an AI-enabled intrusion detection system (IDS) monitors network traffic and analyses the activity of systems and applications and can automatically take action to neutralise malicious behaviour.

AI in Law Enforcement

- **Predictive Policing** - Predictive policing. AI-powered software analyses crime statistics to anticipate the time and location of future criminal activity. This helps pinpoint high-risk areas for law-enforcement resources that can prevent crimes before they happen. The downside is that, like any other AI system, predictive policing can reinforce existing prejudices in the data. We need transparency and fairness to keep public trust with these tools.

- **Facial Recognition** - Authorities can use test images and videos to track suspects, solve crimes and prevent terrorism. This is where AI facial recognition enters the equation. AI powered facial recognition can easily find matching faces in footage video or in a database, serve up notifications in real time. So, using it can enhance the security of the country, but it also raises privacy concerns on a broad scale. Authorities should implement stricter rules and monitoring to prevent misuse of private information and ensure protection of privacy for citizens.

- **AI-Driven Surveillance** - AI will make surveillance faster and more effective, as it is capable of processing enormous amounts of video and audio data. It can do things like detect suspicious behaviour, recognise number plates, and monitor public locations for dangers. We can enhance public safety in such situations but must always align it with ethics and respect for civil liberties. Transparency and accountability in AI-based surveillance is a must to prevent it from being used against civilians.

Benefits of AI in Global Security

- **AI improves big decisions on national defence**, cybersecurity and law enforcement. AI-enriched analytics allows our agencies to make sound decisions, execute proactive responses, and allocate resources. With improved big decision-making, we will have stronger security and defence schemes.

- **Increased Efficiency and Cost Savings** - Routine tasks are automated, thereby freeing up security personnel for more complex or strategy-oriented tasks, like analysing trends revealed by surveillance footage. And of course, AI saves money by automating work. For instance, if an AI system can monitor surveillance footage round-the-clock, officers will be able to focus their work on tasks that they're better equipped for.

- **Proactive Threat Detection** - An AI system can detect threats proactively by flagging hard-to-detect patterns or anomalies that are indicative of security risks, giving agencies a warning and increasing reaction time, as well as allowing them to prevent incidents before they even happen.AI-enabled proactive threat detection, for example, can help detect potential terrorism finance using predictive analytics to identify suspicious financial transactions, potentially preventing the very funding of terrorism.

Challenges and Ethical Considerations

- **Data Privacy and Security** - As AI becomes increasingly important when it comes to global security, the collection and analysis of personal and sensitive information will require strict data protections. Global powers will need to enforce regulations and policies, like the General Data Protection Regulation (GDPR), to address data breaches, which could result in loss of trust from the public.

- **Bias and Fairness** - AI systems will encode whatever bias already exists in their training data; this can lead to unfair treatment and discrimination, as in predictive policing and facial recognition. Developing plans to identify and mitigate bias in algorithms is a critical concern, so that AI systems do not unfairly target people or communities.

- **Autonomous Decision-Making -** The concern lies in questions of accountability. How can we maintain control over autonomous weapons and AI-driven decisions, and avoid causing unforeseen consequences? Developing clear frameworks of ethical conduct for AI will be vital in addressing these issues and ensuring that those implicated in AI-driven actions are held accountable.

- **Regulatory and Legal Issues** - fast-paced innovation of the AI industries creates hurdles in regulatory efforts to create a responsible – ie, ethical and legal – development and use of AI in the context of global security. We need clear regulatory frameworks and guidelines to oversee the development and use of AI technologies. Regulations applied by nation states and institutionally might differ across countries and jurisdictions and become fragmented, making international coordinated collaboration a major goal to harmonise regulatory frameworks and best practices.

Strategies for Balancing Innovation and Risk

- **Developing Robust Ethical Guidelines** - State and International institutions need to create strong ethical frameworks governing AI in global security, such as governing rules to ensure accountability, transparency and human control. Identifying robust ethical parameters and desirable behaviours for the practice of defence is essential to avoid abuse and keep human rights intact.

- **Implementing Strong Regulatory Frameworks** - Regulatory frameworks will need to be established with respect to the development and deployment of AI in security worldwide. These will cover regulations related to privacy expectations for data collection, measures for reducing biases, transparency, and accountability. The UN and other international bodies can help to create a harmonising mechanism within these regulations with respect to best practices.

- **Ensuring Human Oversight** - There must be a human in the loop to avoid unintended consequences and secure oversight in

AI-led decision-making. All autonomous systems must be designed to have built-in fail-safes and means of human intervention. Human responsibility must be made unambiguous so that humans can remain the decision-making authority.

- **Promoting Transparency and Accountability** - Transparency and accountability in the use of AI systems will help establish public trust that they are being deployed in a way consistent with principles of human rights, and not as a means of subverting those rights. This means that government agencies and other officials need to provide information about the use of AI in global security. This could be done efficiently by establishing independent oversight when it comes to the use of AI systems.

- **Investing in AI Research and Development** – Research and development into AI are a key requirement to make sure that AI technologies are safe, reliable and effective. Governments need to fund research into AI ethics, bias detection and privacy-enhancing technologies. This research should be coordinated by global organisations to maximise its influence. Likewise, public policies should incentivise and fund public-private partnerships and collaboration to make sure that AI technologies are innovative and meaningful for real-world security challenges.

Future Directions

- **International Collaboration and Governance** - International cooperation will be necessary to develop responses to the global problems and prospects AI presents for global security. This can include governments co-creating international standards, sharing best practices, coordinating international responses to the international aspects of these technologies (such as cybersecurity and autonomous weapons), and developing international governance arrangements to ensure that AI is used responsibly in the global security context.

- **Advancing AI Ethics Research** - To enhance the ongoing development of frameworks and principles concerning the broader range of AI ethics questions in the context of global security, more research into AI ethics is needed. This research should explore topics relevant to the frameworks, such as accountability, transparency, mitigation of bias, and respect for human rights. The collaborative contribution to AI ethics research of academic, industry and governmental actors would be particularly valuable.

- **Developing Privacy-Preserving Technologies** - AI systems must be accompanied by privacy-preserving technologies to prevent new forms of abuse of legitimate security measures, such as mass surveillance by intelligence services. Techniques such as differential privacy, federated learning and secure multi-party computation can be used to enhance data privacy and security. Governments and industry must heavily invest in such research and development.

- **Fostering Public Trust and Engagement** - Introduction: State leaders need to find ways to promote public understanding and engagement with AI. Institutional embrace of AI is an imperfect proxy for public acceptance and involvement. A multi-track approach – where governments consult with citizens and civil society organisations, and foster awareness and understanding of AI among citizens and residents – is important in building trust and mitigating concerns and anxiety. Again, clear and public communication, including public consultations and participatory approaches, would help governments to explain why specific AI-powered tools are deployed and what citizen and human rights they are intended to protect. This is important because online biases and inequalities will wither only if people can trust that AI-powered systems in global security are accountable, transparent and fair.

Case Studies and Real-World Examples

- **AI in Israel's Iron Dome** – Israel's missile-defence system, known as Iron Dome, relies on AI to identify and neutralise incoming threats. The system uses radar data to distinguish missile trajectories from other signals in the sky, then deploys interceptors precisely in their paths. The proven efficacy of the Iron Dome shows how AI capabilities can be harnessed to bolster national defences.

- **AI in the European Union's Cybersecurity Strategy** - Courtesy the European Union -The EU cybersecurity strategy uses AI to improve detection and response to cyber threats. AI systems identify malicious network traffic patterns; recognise anomalies in those patterns; detect intrusions; determine whether an intrusion included attempts to steal data; and respond to the intrusions by, for example turning off computers in the network. The EU's focus on AI for maintaining cybersecurity and protecting critical infrastructure.

- **AI in the United States' Predictive Policing** - At least three law enforcement agencies in the United States have launched predictive policing programmes, which use AI-powered software to analyse the past incidence of crime and predict future criminal activity. The systems have been deployed in Los Angeles and Chicago, among other cities, to make more efficient use of resources and to curb crimes before they take place. The track record of these programmes serves to highlight both the promise and perils of AI in policing.

- **AI in the United Nations' Peacekeeping Missions** – AI is aiding the work of the United Nations in peacekeeping missions around the world, from combing through information on conflict zones, to extrapolating potentially violent events, to driving decisions on resource usage to improve the impact of missions with more effective means and streamlined resources. AI is helping to keep the peace on a global scale.

Conclusion

Artificial intelligence (AI) is revolutionising global security enhancement of national defence, cybersecurity, and law enforcement. The growing adoption of AI in global security is promising to improve security around the world; however, the risks associated with data privacy, biases, ethical use and regulatory oversight should be considered. Artificial intelligence can automatically trace and analyse patterns from large amounts of data, facilitating better decision making, technology modelling and risk assessment of criminal activity. Consequently, as global data collection expands, national law enforcement agencies will need innovative AI surveillance and targets' profiling capabilities. According to the number of server farms, the allocation of internet bandwidth and the distribution of IP addresses, data brokers, Internet of Things (IoT), and cloud data will accelerate the development of forms of life and work. However, along with the transformation of the world through machine intelligence and cognition, AI will raise data protection, bias, ethical usage, and regulatory concerns.

These same rules must guide its responsible and equitable use. Sound ethical norms baked into robust legislation, enforceable international standards, meaningful human oversight, transparency and accountability can all serve to facilitate innovation while mitigating risk. Strong domestic and international collaboration, robust and expanding AI ethics research, public trust and engagement all can help AI unlock greater benefits for a safer, more secure world.

The way forward will be to continue probing and expanding frontiers in AI in global security, both in theory and in application. We should therefore seek a future in which AI technologies help make significant inroads into the progress of national and international security, and human rights protection.

CHAPTER 10

AI, Privacy, and Surveillance: Balancing Security and Civil Liberties

Introduction

Artificial intelligence (AI) has also dramatically expanded the capacity of governments and organisations to track and gather information in near to real-time. While these new abilities help to secure people and expedite processes, they create potential threats to privacy and civil liberties as well.

This chapter explores how new developments in AI have transformed privacy and surveillance into a double-edged sword that affects applications, benefits, challenges and the strategies required to benefit from its capacity to secure and protect citizens while defending their individual freedoms.

AI in Surveillance

- **Enhanced Monitoring Capabilities** - machine algorithms now make surveillance ever more powerful, fed by new license-plate-recognition cameras, CCTV footage, social media, and other public records. By looking at trends, signatures, maps and faces, AI-based systems are learning to recognise patterns and anomalies, possibly in real time. AI-driven and persistent facial recognition could match, for example, a face to a database of suspects.

- **Predictive Surveillance** – Predictive surveillance applies AI to security threats, monitoring patterns and behaviours in the past and the present to predict criminal behaviour in the future. Machine learning algorithms can monitor for predatory behaviours or patterns that signal an increased likelihood of criminal activity to enable their pre-emptive intervention. For example, predictive analytics can flag unusual transactions that might signal money laundering or terrorist finance and tip off law enforcement.

- **Automated Data Analysis** - AI-assisted analysis of surveillance data frees up human agents from having to monitor everything 24/7 and do it more efficiently. AI systems can scan hours of video footage and notify those agencies about suspicious activities that demand supervision, bringing more actionable intelligence to analysts monitoring the event. This is especially effective in large-scale occasions or areas with multitudes of people.

Benefits of AI in Surveillance

- **Improved Security and Safety** - Automated surveillance gives law enforcement and relevant security agencies timely, relevant and specific information thereby making them more effective as crime preventive agencies. Response time will be faster. Public safety will be much improved. For instance, one terrorist plan for attacks in major cities may have been foiled in Germany recently through AI-driven surveillance of crowds with the identification of suspicious behaviour.

- **Operational Efficiency** - Automating the analysis of surveillance data maximises operational efficiency; freed human resources can be used for more strategic tasks. Skilfully designed AI can analyse and create data much faster than humans, allowing for greater prioritisation of critical information – something that is crucial in high-stress conditions where fast decision-making is essential.

- **Cost-Effective Solutions** - AI helps cut down costs: Surveillance without the labour-intensive processes of data monitoring and human analysis is cheaper to implement. Some were originally developed under Nazi rule and later been co-opted for commercial use in the US, with massive funding from the Department of Defence. At lower costs, massive data collection and monitoring becomes economically feasible for large numbers of companies and governments. That means enhanced surveillance infrastructure.

Challenges and Ethical Considerations

- **Privacy Invasion** – As the case of AI-based surveillance demonstrates, one of the great fears about this technology is that it involves an invasion of privacy. If surveillance is all-encompassing and eavesdropping happens on a mass scale, then the right to privacy will be compromised and society will develop a culture where people routinely feel they are being watched. The principle of proportionality of surveillance measures would need to be respected in such cases to prevent abuses.

- **Bias and Discrimination** - AI systems can inherit all kinds of biases from the training data with which they're exposed; and these biases can, in turn, be extended into discriminatory policing. Vince Warren of the Centre for Constitutional Rights in New York says that current facial recognition technology has high error rates for people of colour and for women. The responses to these buts are crucial to legitimising AI surveillance systems and to mitigating tendencies towards recreating and replicating existing inequalities – or generating new ones.

- **Transparency and Accountability** - The black box nature of the algorithms that underpin AI make it difficult to assess or verify what's happening, either in terms of transparency or accountability. For example, a surveillance system might not be transparent, in that citizens don't know how it's being used; or it could lack accountability because we don't have any formal means of holding those in power to account for their use of it.

- **Legal and Regulatory Issues** - The stepwise spread of AI in surveillance well exceeds following the evolution of legal and regulatory frameworks. Needed are also clear rules governing the use of AI in surveillance, at least concerning the collection, storage and use of data. International cooperation can help to harmonise regulations and make them based on general standards.

Balancing Security and Civil Liberties

- **Developing Robust Privacy Laws -** They should also introduce firm privacy legislation involving set limits on AI's ability to collect and use data, clear rules defining what their governments can do, and methods for recourse if those authorities overstep. Mirroring the GDPR can help them.

- **Implementing Privacy-Preserving Technologies** - Privacy-preserving technologies (for example, differential privacy and federated learning) strike a good trade-off between security and privacy: it's possible to carry out statistical analysis on data without having to see individuals' micro-data. Differential privacy 'disguises' data with a certain level of noise, so that it's impossible to extract individuals' micro-data when aggregating information.

Federated learning allows the carrying out of an analysis of data without the need to have all the information concentrated in one spot (e.g., switching to an Amazon Warehouse from an Amazon shop). To put it differently: online surveillance without the need for a man-in-the-middle.

- **Ensuring Transparency and Public Oversight** - In the interest of public trust, information about state surveillance should be transparent, and made readily available. What kinds of data are AI systems collecting, and for what purposes are these data used? Better surveillance practices can be enforced when public oversight bodies monitor and/or intervene in the activities of the state.

- **Addressing Bias and Ensuring Fairness** - Avoiding bias in AI surveillance systems: avoid anarchy, keep the peace Many people are concerned that lobby groups not directly impacted by police oversight are increasingly influencing surveillance policy, so to ensure there is accurate and unbiased AI surveillance, the training sets should be diverse and representative, and regular audits should identify and remedy biases among different groups. Governments and citizens can take action to support AI systems that prioritise the protection of vulnerable communities and promote social equity.

- **Promoting Ethical AI Development** – Responsible development of AI should include ways to embed ethical decisions and concerns into the process of AI being designed, developed and deployed. For instance, this means thinking about developing a framework of ethical guidelines, undertaking AI-related impact assessments, and developing a community that is sensitive towards these issues and includes forms of responsibility among those building technologies. When surveillance technologies are integrated in responsible ways, they can be used to advance human rights and the public good.

Future Directions

- **Advancing Privacy-Preserving AI Resea** - Exploring the frontiers of privacy-preserving AI techniques, such as innovations in homomorphic encryption, secure multi-party computation and privacy-preserving machine learning, could help build algorithms that ensure both individual privacy rights and the ability of law enforcement officials to accomplish their tasks effectively.

- **Strengthening International Collaboration** - Creating international standards on limits and uses of AI-driven surveillance is essential. Pooling our resources on developing international regimes, meeting regularly to share best practices, and offering coordinated responses to cross-border issues like cybercrime and terrorism are major avenues for collaboration. Sharing neighbour's blame only extends so far. Going through life with reasonably low expectations is what allows many in the Western world to get along with others that are like them. This strategy of moderation limits the amount of outrage that can be directed towards foreigners, and it shields people from having to take actions that don't align with their other priorities.

- **Empowering Citizens through Digital Literacy** - Citizens need better digital literacy than they currently have, so that they understand their rights, and know what is coming and what it will mean for them. Schools and universities can provide training, and government agencies can run public advertising campaigns to educate citizens. When people know what is going on and why, they will be better able to speak up for their own rights: to choose whether they want their data flywheels to spin, and to define their own privacy rights. They can then participate in debates on surveillance and privacy in the public sphere.

- **Implementing Adaptive Regulatory Frameworks** - Regulations regarding AI-driven surveillance should be flexible, as technologies evolve too quickly to create rigid rules. Governments must create forward-thinking regulation that allows for the fluctuation of technological capabilities while maintaining fundamental human rights and understandings of civil liberty. Laws should be regularly reviewed and updated.

- **Fostering Ethical AI Communities** - Communities of practice can be formed around the concept of ethical AI, and they can shape the development and use of surveillance technologies. Academics, industry, government and civil society can get together to exchange knowledge, address challenges related to ethical including in AI surveillance practices and develop tools and resources.

Case Studies and Real-World Examples

- **AI in Smart City Surveillance** – Many smart cities are using AI-powered surveillance systems to enhance urban security and efficiency. For instance, AI-enhanced cameras monitor public spaces and promote safety in Singapore. Moreover, AI optimises traffic and signals, and detects anomalies. Despite the safety and operational efficiency these technologies grant, privacy and data security are issues. Singapore shows that smart cities should include transparent governance and robust privacy protections.

- **Facial Recognition in Law Enforcement** - The use of facial recognition technology by agencies like the Metropolitan Police in London has been controversial. While facial recognition can be a valuable tool to track suspects and solve crimes, it also raises important privacy issues and potential bias in relation to the technology. Procedure needs to be transparent, accountable and just to build public trust and civil liberty.

- **AI in Predictive Policing** - Predictive policing programmes, like those in Chicago and Los Angeles, apply AI to historical crime data, analysing it to foretell where future crime might occur. Although they are meant to help police departments better allocate resources and stop crime before it occurs, predictive policing systems have attracted controversies over the biases they produce and the way their models can single out already marginalised individuals and communities. This requires immediate consideration and action to redress the inbuilt bias and promote fairness when employing predictive policing.

- **AI in Border Security** - Surveillance, particularly due to AI, is used at the border to better control immigration flows. For example, the US Customs and Border Protection (CBP) uses AI to analyse data flows such as video footage and biometric information to improve border security. The tension between protecting the border and complying with principles of privacy and respect for individual rights is important in the use of AI at the border.

Conclusion

AI-powered surveillance promises advantages in terms of increasing security, maximising operational efficiency and providing cost-effective solutions. At the same time, these systems pose their own set of challenges, including issues of privacy transgression, bias, transparency and lack of regulatory oversight. While security and civil liberties cannot be considered as mutually exclusive issues, can we find ways to achieve a balance in our approach to AI-driven surveillance? The answer undeniably lies in developing sound privacy laws, enhancing privacy-preserving technologies, ensuring transparency and public oversight, tackling the issue of bias, and prioritising ethical AI development. Future research that might prove to be useful for ensuring safeguards for personal freedoms using AI-driven surveillance can be found in the development of privacy-preserving AI technologies; international collaboration for addressing challenges and tackling risks; utilising digital literacy to empower citizens in enforcing their rights; maximising the efficiency of adaptive regulatory frameworks to combat the multifaceted problems caused due to AI-driven surveillance; and fostering the development of ethical communities to ensure the safeguarding of human rights and societal wellbeing. To conclude, while these challenges might appear daunting, AI in the sphere of surveillance holds tremendous potential for security and operational efficiency.

CHAPTER 11

AI and Social Equity: Bridging the Gap

Introduction

AI can help to close or widen social gaps, depending on how AI is developed and deployed Artificial intelligence has the potential to reduce or widen social gaps, depending on how it is developed and deployed. On the positive side, AI can improve access to housing, education, healthcare and jobs; but it can also reinforce and even exacerbate existing gaps, unless careful attention is given to how AI technologies are designed and used. In this chapter I discuss what AI technologies can be used for in the field of social equity, what advantages they bring, what challenges they generate, and how such technologies can best be deployed 'for the people' to make our world more inclusive, fair and just.

AI in Education

- **Enhancing Access to Quality Education** – Educational technologies that use AI can democratise education. Up-to-date, high-quality educational experiences can be pushed to students via platforms such as Khan Academy or Coursera, where students from geographically or economically disadvantaged settings can receive the same high-quality educational resources as those from advantaged backgrounds.

- **Addressing Learning Disabilities** - AI can offer students with learning disabilities tailored learning plans and tools that fit with students' needs. For instance, AI-based apps such as Microsoft's Immersive Reader can help students with dyslexia format and structure the text so that they can easily read, as well as providing audio text as it is accessed. These tools can be transformative to help students access their learning to its fullest potential.

- **Reducing Dropout Rates** - Predictive analytics using AI can identify students who are at risk of dropping out (based on their attendance rate, grades, scoring patterns, engagement etc) and suggest interventions that could flatten the dropout curve and the STEM dropout gap. Through outreach, coaching and remediation, these students can be pushed towards the degree. Programs such as the one at Georgia State, which leverages predictive analytics, has shown significant reduction in dropout rates, across all student groups, and increased graduation rates.

AI in Healthcare

- **Improving Access to Healthcare Services** - AI socially empower populations that are especially challenged to access health services. Whether they live in a remote area of an emerging health jurisdiction, or in a developed country, digital health assistants such as phone- or chat-based virtual assistants could offer a first contact with a healthcare system incapable of physically delivering healthcare services. For populations with spotty access to basic health facilities, we could significantly improve health outcomes through delivery of core clinical services promised by human health workers.

- **Personalized Treatment Plans** - For instance, by allowing personalised medicine, in which individual data on a patient are analysed to provide tailored treatment programmes for each person, and thereby ensure that people who are diagnosed with often fatal diseases get the treatment that is most likely to cure their form of the disease, such as using AI through IBM Watson Health to analyse large amounts of medical data and suggest the best personalised treatment for those who suffer from cancer.

- **Addressing Health Disparities** - Artificial intelligence can help providers recognise health inequities by conducting research on social determinants of health, such as socioeconomic status, education and environment; doing so would allow intervention initiatives that target interventions for the benefit of marginalized populations. Moreover, AI can analyse data for clues as to how best to help – it can suggest research questions and notice patterns that further inform us of strategies to attenuate health disparities.

AI in Employment

- **Promoting Inclusive Hiring Practices** - AI can reduce bias in the hiring process by focusing only on candidates' skill levels and qualifications, rather than problematic additional factors such as gender, race, or socioeconomic background. For example, platforms such as Hire Vue use an AI-powered hiring platform to record candidates' responses and use this information combined with virtual simulations to assess candidates based on objective information, in addition to subjective skills and technical measures. The greatest concern is ensuring that the algorithms themselves are created to be non-discriminatory.

- **Supporting Workforce Development** – in regard to workforce development, AI can identify skills mismatches and prescribe new training regimens to help workers develop the capabilities they need to function in new roles, including industry-specific platforms such as LinkedIn Learning that will personalise learning plans for workers to gain the skills they need in the marketplace; – for displaced or underemployed workers, this type of AI can help accelerate their transition to new jobs and improve their economic prospects (hopefully improving their sense of self-worth as well).

- **Enhancing Workplace Accessibility** - AI can increase the workplace accessibility to ensure that it is a safe and welcoming space for all employees. For employees with disabilities, speech-to-text AI applications can transcribe audio notes from meetings and dictate word processing documents. For employees with visual impairments, AI-powered screen readers can help them access digital information in various formats.

AI in Economic Opportunity

- **Financial Inclusion** – But also, using AI to enhance financial inclusion. Finance platforms such as Tala that use machine learning to provide loans to less-banked populations based on alternative data, making banking and other financial services available to more people, are a good example.

- **Supporting Small and Medium Enterprises (SMEs)** - Through targeted tools for market analysis, customer insights, and operational efficiency, AI can help small and medium enterprises (SMEs) to grow and develop. AI-powered tools can help SMEs manage their supply chains, their money, and develop targeted marketing strategies. With the help of AI, SMEs can compete on a more equal footing with larger corporations and provide much-needed stimulus to the economy.

- **Enhancing Agricultural Productivity** - AI can help agriculture become more productive and sustainable by providing farmers with data-driven guidance. For example, Farm Logs, a website using satellite imagery and machine learning, can analyse soil health, weather and crop information to suggest that farmers irrigate their crops or use insecticides. If more farmers can use these tools, it could lead to better yields, fewer resources used, and more secure food for communities.

Challenges and Ethical Considerations

1. **Bias in AI Algorithms** - Secondly, bias in algorithms is a real concern in the race to achieve effective artificial intelligence. The problem is that algorithms can reflect and amplify inequalities in society. By ensuring that AI systems are trained with as detailed and representative datasets as possible, these problems can be lessened or mitigated. Audits of how algorithms are designed and regular assessments of their fairness are also helpful.

2. **Digital Divide** – The digital divide continues to be a major reason why AI adoptions will be inequitable: access to and digital literacy is unevenly distributed, and this means that the most marginalised segments of society will be left behind. To address the digital divide will require greater investments in infrastructure, education and policies that ensure that technology is accessible to everyone.

3. **Privacy Concerns** - It relies on the widespread collection and analysis of data, a practice that might raise concerns about privacy and data safety. The use of AI may at times interfere with

protections set by existing legislation, and researchers and industry leaders should strive to abide by robust data protection regulations such as the General Data Protection Regulation (GDPR), as well as recognise and respect each person's right to privacy. Practising transparent data collection and getting the informed consent of citizens for the use of their data are vital aspects of the ethical use of AI.

4. **Economic Displacement** - While the coming of AI might lead to new job creation, it could also entail economic displacement as automation substitutes for certain jobs. Reskilling and upskilling programmes, robust social safety nets, and policies supporting workforce transitions will all be needed to navigate this challenge. It is imperative that the benefits arising from AI remain shared by as many people as possible, or risk fostering growing economic divides.

Strategies for Promoting Social Equity through AI

- **Inclusive AI Development** - Stakeholder engagement helps develop inclusive AI by fully engaging the people, communities and groups that are impacted by, using, using or developing AI technology – incorporating diverse stakeholders in the design, development and deployment of AI systems, such as traditionally underrepresented communities in technology development such as women, people of colour, and those with disabilities or marginalised groups Collaborative approaches drive inclusive AI through engaging and developing it in dialogue with all groups.

- **Ethical AI Frameworks** – Principled ethical systems for AI need to be in place. These should allow for the principled development and use of AI. They could include principles such as fairness, transparency, traceability, accountability, responsible use, inclusivity, and respect for intellectual property and privacy. Industry, government and civil society can work together to develop activity and evaluation systems that define and assess the extent to which AI technologies adhere to formal principles.

- **Public Awareness and Education** - Increasing public understanding of AI can help citizens understand its promise and its limitations and equip them to participate to the fullest in decision-making about these important technologies. Education programmes and public information campaigns can help to alert citizens to AI's power and to arm them with the knowledge and skills to engage critically with it, and even to be alert to the situation where they need to have their rights protected by the state. Paywall-free, open-access, peer-reviewed research: www.TandFonline.com/cognition

- **Policy and Regulation** - To work for social equity, governments need to be involved in ensuring that AI technologies are designed properly by issuing policies and regulations on the potential harms and biases, as well as on the economic displacements that new technologies create. Regulatory frameworks would be iterative, improving and developing when used and adapted to shape policy goals on a country-by-country basis. Governments then would promote social goods and improve social lives, ensuring that these technologies were used for the greater good.

- **Collaboration and Partnerships** – governments, the private sector, academia and civil society need to work together to promote social equity through AI. Strong public-private partnerships can stimulate innovation, share best practices, and develop solutions to complex problems. Inclusive collaboration to develop and deploy AI will ensure systems are developed and deployed in a way that benefits all members of society.

Future Directions

- **AI for Social Good** - The problems that we'll try to fix with AI have to go beyond 'How do we make Google better?'. There are many important social goodness problems for AI to help us solve like poverty and inequality and climate change. AI for social good can help us direct the technology to solve the problems we care about overall.

- **Investing in Human-Centric AI Research** - A Symbiotic Scheme Invest in basic research on human-centric AI Donate to universities conducting initiatives such as the HCI colloquium to promote research on technologies that foster positive human experiences, while discouraging those that diminish them. Fund basic research on notions of humanness that are oriented around social equity, and invest in facilitating research on ethical AI, fairness in AI algorithms, and privacy-preserving technologies. Nurture research collaboration among governments, industry and academia.

- **Global Collaboration for Inclusive AI** - International cooperation will be essential to help guarantee that AI technologies are not exclusionary or stratifying: global institutions can support sharing of resources, knowledge and best practices across countries. Joint work can help address global challenges such as the digital divide and economic inequality and promote AI that is used in a manner that enhances our ability to meet human needs responsibly everywhere.

- **Empowering Communities through AI** – Assisting communities with AI means giving them the skills and means to use AI for their own benefit, such as training programmes, technology access and support for homegrown AI projects. Enabled communities can shape AI and use it to best suit their needs to solve local problems, enhance their lives, and create progress for society overall.

Case Studies and Real-World Examples

- **AI in India's Education Sector** - Byju's and other AI-powered teaching platforms are making quality education available to tens of millions of lower-middle and lower-income Indian students, including those in remote and underserved regions of the country. The success of Byju's shows that AI can decrease educational inequality.

- **AI in Rwanda's Healthcare System** – Rwanda is using AI to extend quality healthcare to its rural patients by employing telemedicine platforms powered by AI algorithms that connect remotely, providing consultations and diagnostics that improve health outcomes and reduce primary healthcare disparities.

- **AI in Brazil's Financial Inclusion Efforts** - In Brazil, for example, financial inclusion is being promoted via AI-powered banking platforms such as Nu bank, a new generation neo-bank backed by the Nasdaq-listed payments company Stone Co. Starting from the premise that traditional data sources such as credit reports are both incomplete and biased, Nu bank uses AI to assess creditworthiness according to new alternative data. This allows even those without a credit history to gain access to the financial system. As a result, the gap between Brazil's banked and unbanked population keeps narrowing.

- **AI in Kenya's Agricultural Sector** - For example, artificial intelligence (AI) is boosting agricultural production in Kenya through platforms such as Farm Drive, which processes data to help farmers make smart decisions, from tracking soil health and weather patterns to monitoring crop conditions. Since starting, Farm Drive has helped farmers improve yields, reduce resource use, and has boosted the food security of local communities.

Conclusion

Such an AI can honour social equity and equal opportunity in education, health, employment, and economic opportunity. So how do we get there? Meeting the challenges of bias, privacy, the digital divide and economic displacement will unleash AI for social equity. To do this we'll need to focus on inclusive AI development; ethical, legal and policy guidelines for AI; public awareness and education; policy and regulation; and collaboration and partnerships. The most heartening lesson of history is the knowledge that humans can and do change as we witness chapters like this. AI technologies can generate a more inclusive and equitable society ahead, if we rigorously pursue the paths of exploration, innovation and persistence in AI for social equity.

CHAPTER 12

*The Psychological Impact of AI:
Navigating Human-AI Interactions*

Introduction

One of the most intriguing questions regarding human-technology interaction is how the increasing presence of artificial intelligence (AI) in our daily lives will shape minds and societies in the years and decades to come. If, as is widely expected, the next contentious debate over the meaning of mental and emotional wellbeing will unfold within the context of human-artificial intelligence (AI) interaction, what are the psychological consequences likely to be? How will humans maintain positive mental health and emotional wellbeing? How will social interactions between people and AI will play out? What opportunities does this new world give rise to, as well as inherent dangers? Those are the questions this chapter will seek to address, discussing both potential problems and opportunities within the context of psychological issues such as mental health, human-AI relationships and possible social isolation, and how to manage adverse consequences and enhance the positive ones.

AI and Mental Health

- **AI-Powered Mental Health Support** - AI technologies are being used to develop virtual therapists and chatbots and mental health apps. These AI tools take away the barriers that sometimes stand between people and getting mental health care such as cost or location. For instance, chatbots such as Warbot and Wyse allow users to talk to AI avatars backed by natural language processing abilities that can deliver cognitive-behavioural therapy techniques and provide emotional support.

- **Early Detection of Mental Health Issues** - AI might identify mental health problems often before a patient seeks medical attention, thanks to machine learning algorithms can figure out patterns of behaviour (and wording) by analyzing social media content and data gathered from smart wearables and digital footprint. For example, the latest IBM cognitive approach can detect mental-health conditions such as depression, anxiety and PTSD before even the patient believe has a problem. This in turn may lead to early intervention and support – and even avoid mental health issues from deteriorating.

- **Personalized Mental Health Interventions** - Artificial intelligence (AI) can also support increasingly personalised mental health interventions by reviewing individual data and shaping treatment plans to suit an individual's needs. Facebook, for example, has developed AI-driven mental health platforms that recommend personalised coping methods, customised mindfulness exercises and targeted therapy based on an individual user's behaviour and interests. By personalising the intervention, individuals with mental health needs may find the intervention to be more effective over the long term.

Human-AI Relationships

- **Emotional Attachment to AI** – As the technological capabilities of AI increase, and become more human-like, interpersonal attachments might develop to AI entities. Virtual assistants, such as Siri or Alexa; and social robots, such as the Japanese robot Pepper, are intended to have characteristics that elicit emotional reactions. Although people can derive benefits from these attachments, such as having a companion or a helper, they also raise questions about what it means to be in a relationship, or to be emotionally dependent on a computer.

- **AI as Companions -** Besides creating personalised artistic content, there are other recent uses of AI. AI companions – a virtual friend, a robot pet – are increasingly used to combat loneliness and provide emotional support. Examples include robotic pets such as Sony's AIBO, or a digital virtual friend like Replika.

- **Ethical Considerations of AI Relationships** – What are the ethical implications of developing emotional relationships with AI entities? Protections and questions for AI-user relationships include ensuring authenticity, informed consent and no manipulation. Designing sexual relations is problematic, but designing emotional relations may be even more so. What are the guardrails here? Are there guidelines that can be used to judge if the AI-user relationship is designed to be exploitative or supportive? What does a real, informed, consensual emotional relationship with an AI entity look like? In AI-human relations, guardrails must be developed in the hope that these entities are as sensitive, responsive and ethical as possible.

Social Isolation and AI

- **AI-Induced Social Isolation** – Even though AI can be a source of support and comfort, there might be cause for concern that an increase in AI engagement could lead to social isolation. People may begin to turn to AI for more and more of their interactions and thus become more isolated from family, friends and community. Decreased social interaction could harm mental health and lead to poor social integration.

- **Balancing AI and Human Interactions** – Balance your AI interactions with human relationships before social isolation sets in. While AI technologies may someday become more advanced than humans, in general it is important to design human-machine interactions to complement rather than replace human relationships. Encouraging users to maintain human relationships play a vital role in helping to mitigate the risk of AI-induced isolation.

- **AI in Social Connectivity** - Similarly, it can augment social connectivity through communication channels and socialising platforms. AI-driven technologies such as Zoom and social media algorithms can be used to stay in touch with friends and family, organise virtual celebrations and form online communities, which in turn can support individuals' social lives and foster a sense of belonging.

Strategies for Positive Psychological Outcomes

- **Promoting Digital Literacy and Awareness** - Since AI will likely have psychological effects, these must be made known to pre-emptively build healthy relationships. Digital literacy programmes can educate users about the strengths and weaknesses of using AI so that they can shape their own use of the technology. Awareness campaigns can help to prepare people about tensions that might arise from too much time on their screens or from allowing too much interaction with robots.

- **Designing Human-Centric AI** - Developing human-centric AI means prioritising human wellbeing and needs in the design of artificial intelligence technologies. To do this, the technologies need to be designed in a way that enhances users' mental health, helps them to foster social bonds, and supports their emotional wellbeing. Humane AI would ensure that technology serves to uplift, rather than to distract and diminish, human life.

- **Implementing Ethical AI Guideline** - Creating ethical guidelines for the responsible development and deployment of AI technologies is key. How can we protect against emotional manipulation, or establish norms around consent and authenticity online? Guidelines and agreed practices need to be in place to protect the psychological wellbeing of users on online platforms. Policymakers will need to work with developers and ethicists to create the frameworks that both allow AI technologies to flourish, while ensuring that their use remains responsible and ethical.

- **Encouraging Responsible AI Use** – Value-building forms of encouragement include encouraging responsible AI use for good psychological outcomes, creating appropriate limits on screen time and comfort with AI interactions, adopting mental health behaviours and practices that incorporate AI, respecting human connections over AI connections, and seeking professional mental health support when AI is being used in support of negative behaviours. Value-building encouragement guides users to use AI for augmenting relationships or developing new ones, rather than replacing them.

Future Directions

- **Advancing AI in Mental Health Research** - Further research in the use of AI in mental health could lead to new insights and innovations in mental health support, such as the development of more advanced AI-based therapies, advances in early detection algorithms, consideration about the longer-term impact of AI interactions on mental health, and so forth. Continued collaboration between researchers, clinicians and technologists in this area will be key to such progress.

- **Developing AI for Emotional Intelligence** - While we often talk vaguely about making AI more emotional, what is really needed is to develop systems that can interpret and respond with human emotional intelligence. This means improving natural language processing, emotion recognition, and empathetic responses. Users will find emotionally intelligent AI easier and more meaningful to engage with.

- **Exploring Human-AI Coexistence** - We must learn how-to live-in human-AI coexistence. Defined as the 'interaction between humans and artificial intelligence where neither the human nor the AI is negated or oppressed', and evoking 'visions of companionship, complementarity and co-flourishing', human-AI coexistence means examining how human existence can be improved by AI, without becoming exploitative or cause dependence, how human-AI relations create expectations, challenge norms and rituals, what effective best practices of human-AI interaction are and how they unfold, and how AI-enabled technologies can serve as 'instruments of human flourishing'. Exploring human-AI coexistence would inform the future development of AI.

- **Integrating AI in Community and Social Services** - Embedding AI in community services and community-based organisations to supplement how people assist each other can improve the resources and support available to communities and those in need. In this way, residents and community organisations can respond to real-time and future needs that might result from labour shortages, new technology, changing daily demands and routines, and health and wellbeing problems, among other scenarios. By incorporating AI into community and social services, social workers, counsellors and community organisers can be augmented to provide better data-driven insights, perform otherwise time-intensive administrative tasks, and adapt the nature and duration of interventions to each individual's scope of needs, interests and goals. This will improve the social services provided to communities and enable them to thrive.

Case Studies and Real-World Examples

- **Warbot: AI in Mental Health Support** - Woe bot is a cognitive-behavioural therapy-based artificial intelligence-powered chatbot designed to help people cope with issues such as mild depression; users converse with Warbot, who provides them with personalised coping techniques, mood monitoring and emotional support. Woe bot shows the increasing potential for AI in the provision of mental health care.

- **Replica: AI Companionship** - Replica is an AI-based emotional confidant. Available via smartphone, she functions as a surrogate friend or companion with whom users can converse, and who also learns from conversation and provides tailored responses. Replica helps people combat loneliness and can act as an emotional support. Her existence raises important questions about the ethics of forming emotional relationships with AI.

- **Sony AIBO: Robotic Pets -** Sony's robotic pet AIBO is designed to follow and play with its owner, acknowledge commands and mimic human-like behaviour, interacting in predictable and warm ways. The success of AIBO as a companion and toy hints at the real possibility that AI-enabled robotic friends may one day serve as effective emotional supports for combating loneliness.

- **Zoom: AI in Social Connectivity** - The digital communications platform Zoom employs AI to improve videoconferencing that encourages relationships and social connectivity. Its AI features, such as muting out background noise, live transcription and automatic scheduling provide seamless virtual interactions that keep people more connected. Zoom became a mainstay during the coronavirus shutdowns that confined people to home quarantines.

Conclusion

The question of how AI might affect mental health and society is not easy to answer: there are so many different dimensions. AI could help mental health support to be better tailored and more widely available to different populations; it could help combat loneliness and find new ways of connecting with people who lack social networks; it could help people with cognitive impairments live more independently or provide useful companionship for those in need. However, these balanced forms of AI might come at a significant social cost, because technology has the potential to have negative side-effects that result in digital inequalities, including addiction, reduced social interaction and lower privacy.

Measures such as the promotion of digital literacy, decision-making about human-centric AI, and ethical guidelines for use and implementation should be encouraged. Practicing and disseminating responsible AI, alongside further research, interdisciplinary collaboration, and dialogue, are needed for AI technologies to enhance psychological well-being.

It is critical that human needs – our psychological and emotional well-being – take centre stage in the design, implementation and use of AI technologies from now on. Human-centred design, ethical considerations and responsible use of AI can earn our trust and capitalise on the power of AI to complement, enhance and enrich human processes, so we can work towards a future where AI and humans live in harmony.

CHAPTER 13

The Rise of Autonomous Systems:
Implications for Society

Introduction

With the swift ascendance of artificial intelligence (AI), the idea of autonomous systems is taking shape in many domains, including transport, manufacturing, healthcare, services and a whole range of other areas: systems that can perform tasks on their own volition, without human intervention is the 'new horizon'. Such a shift towards work smarter (or at least devoid of humans), would alert many sets of stakeholders (investors, entrepreneurs and, of course, governments) and hence would usher in an imperative shift from mere products to systems centred around services and outcomes. That said, there are clearly challenges of ethics, legality and societal impact to come into play once the adaptation process starts. In this chapter, I present the emergence of autonomous systems, their applications and contexts, the perceived benefits and challenges, and the societal challenges expected to be induced from such widespread adoption of autonomous systems.

Autonomous Vehicles

1. **Self-Driving Cars** - Perhaps the most familiar application of autonomous systems is in self-driving cars, and several companies including Waymo, Tesla and Uber are developing vehicles that can drive without a human at the wheel. Such cars reply on a network of sensors and cameras that feed information into an artificial-intelligence algorithm with the goal of making decisions about their surroundings and controlling their actions so that they drive themselves and so that accidents are reduced, cars drive more fuel efficiently, and those unable to drive (perhaps because they are too young or too old) can still drive themselves.

2. **Autonomous Public Transport** - Other autonomous systems

are also starting to play a part in public transportation. Autonomous buses, trams and trains can be operated without a driver, and the addition of autonomous vehicles to public transport networks could increase their efficiency and reliability. Cities such as Singapore and Helsinki have begun testing autonomous buses to enhance urban mobility and reduce congestion.

3. **Ethical and Safety Concerns** - Critical decision-making involves ethical dilemmas, such as avoiding an accident involving multiple human lives by preferring to harm human witnesses, or programming differential moral duty obligations depending on gender, ableism or religion. Granting human-like rights to autonomous machines raises concerns about their reliability and safely. This suggests a need for prudent testing and regulatory oversight.

Autonomous Systems in Manufacturing

- **Robotic Automation** - Autonomous robots are revolutionising manufacturing by completing repetitive, dangerous and labour-intensive tasks more precisely and quickly than humans can. 'Collaborative robots', or co-bots, work with human workers to improve their productivity and safety; they can, for example, assemble products, handle materials or conduct quality control. Companies such as Fanuc and Universal Robots design and produce industrial robots that increase the efficiency of production processes.

- **Smart Factories** - By integrating autonomous systems, the IoT and AI, governments could have smart factories that are highly automated and flexible. These smart factories could optimise production in real time, predict maintenance needs and adapt to fluctuations in demand (from varying customer preferences to bulk orders for short durations only). Smart factories can mitigate wastage and downtime for a more efficient, sustainable production process.

Impact on Employment

Such anxieties are understandable only if you don't recognise that the advent of autonomous new systems in manufacturing doesn't mean that we'd be getting rid of manual jobs whilst creating jobs only in, say, maintenance of robots, programming and supervision – not least because those jobs won't involve manual labour. Addressing the burning issue of economic displacement of workers will require pre-emptive re-skilling and up-skilling programmes for preparing the population to fill new roles in the new economy which awaits workers who are relieved of the drudgery of mindless repetition.

- **Autonomous Systems in Health Surgical Robots** – The da Vinci Surgical System is an autonomous medical robot that augments surgeons by giving them greater precision and control over difficult surgical procedures. These systems enhance the ability of surgeons, minimise the possibility for complications, and improve the quality of care for patients. Autonomous and semi-autonomous surgical robots can also support minimally invasive surgeries, allowing for faster recovery times in patients.

- **AI-Powered Diagnostics** - Autonomous diagnostic systems can employ machine-learning models to examine medical images, laboratory results and clinical data for reliable diagnoses. They can spot signs of troublesome conditions such as cancers, cardio-vascular disease and neurological disorders before they become serious. The use of AI diagnostics improves the accuracy and speed of medical assessments, allowing clinicians to offer early support and improved outcomes.

- **Patient Monitoring and Care** – Rather than relying on a few nurses walking around a ward cheerleading, looking at screens and listening to the radio to juggle the needs of 20 or more patients, autonomous systems can collect data on vital signs, drug regimen adherence and overall wellness around the clock. At the same time, AI-powered virtual nurses, like those created by Sense.ly, can speak with patients and managers in a software that uniquely characterises the patient to apply their training and help manage their chronic conditions. These systems can improve patient care, reduce hospital readmissions, and provide a more efficient way of delivering healthcare.

Autonomous Systems in Service Industries

- **Retail and Hospitality** - Increasingly, autonomous systems will cater to customers independently, customising the experience and enhancing operations. Autonomous robots can serve customers, serve food, and even clean up after them. For example, hotels such as YOTEL and Aloft already feature robotic concierges that hand-deliver room service and assist with checking in and checking out, minimising wait time and enhancing guest satisfaction.

- **Agriculture** - There's no doubt that autonomous systems in agriculture – autonomous tractors, grass-harvesting robots, unmanned aerial vehicles (drones) – increase productivity as well as sustainability. Drones can survey the health of crops, spray pesticides and manage irrigation systems; autonomous tractors and other autonomous harvesters can plant, weed and harvest. Labour costs, resource use and alternative crop production all decrease.

- **Logistics and Delivery** - Autonomous systems are disrupting operations in the logistics and delivery sectors by enabling faster and more efficient transportation of goods. For instance, autonomous delivery robots and drones can transport packages, food and other supplies. Autonomous delivery offers new opportunities for Amazon, UPS and other companies to enhance their supply chain capabilities and to match growing consumer demands.

Benefits of Autonomous Systems

- **Increased Efficiency and Productivity** – Autonomous systems promote efficiency and enhance productivity by automating repetitive and time-consuming menial tasks to free up more complex, innovative tasks for humans. This can lead to knowledge-based innovations – a major driver of economic growth. The additional efficiency can also lead to lower costs and increased production for most if not all industries.

- **Improved Safety and Reliability** - Autonomous systems can improve safety by reducing the risk of human error in critical tasks. For instance, autonomous vehicles can minimise traffic accidents due to distracted or impaired driving. In manufacturing, autonomous robots can perform hazardous tasks, which can reduce workplace injuries. The reliability in autonomous systems can ensure the repeatable performance and quality.

- **Enhanced Accessibility** - Autonomous systems can improve accessibility by expanding the services available to people with disabilities or limited mobility. For example, autonomous vehicles could provide transportation to people who cannot drive, and AI-powered virtual assistants could help people live independently, especially the elderly. These systems can help a wide population be more inclusive and live better lives.

Challenges and Ethical Considerations

1. **Regulatory and Legal Issues** - Autonomous systems pose regulatory challenges, not just because they involve a broad range of products and services, but also because existing regulations fail to address many of the issues such systems present – governments will need to quickly develop new regulatory regimes, formulating laws and industry standards aimed at making autonomous systems safe, reliable and ethically sound. Tesla drivers' unexpected difficulty in driving Electric Automation's cars without their Autopilot modes cutting in is one reason why governments must specifically regulate and standardise autonomous systems, to create a level playing field.

2. **Ethical Decision-Making** - Either way, autonomous systems need to be programmed to make ethical decisions in life-and-death situations. Moral dilemmas abound in accident scenarios (Do you sacrifice three people to avoid hitting four that you could

swerve to avoid?) and resource-allocation questions (Who gets cared for by healthcare robots first – the unconscious or the conscious patient?). Developing autonomous systems that conform to societal values and ethical norms demands interdisciplinary work and open decision-making processes.

3. **Privacy and Security Concerns** - The full operation of autonomous systems often requires the gathering and processing of large amounts of data. This can lead to important questions about privacy and security, and appropriate data protection standards must therefore be established and robustly followed (e.g., adherence to European Union's General Data Protection Regulation (GDPR)). Autonomous systems should be developed in ways that both minimise the risk of data breaches, and guarantee data protection mechanisms that safeguard user privacy.

4. **Economic and Social Impacts** - Notwithstanding the accelerating pace of machine learning, autonomous systems are likely to disrupt economies and societies through the mass displacement of workers, changes in employment patterns and flows, and shifts in economic and social power. Societies must proactively avoid sticky transitions as they 'reskill' affected employees; introduce global social safety nets; and empower enterprise transformation so that the gains of AI are more broadly shared than the gains of the Industrial Revolution.

Strategies for Responsible Development and Deployment

- **Developing Ethical Framework** - Moral codes need to be formulated in advance to guide the design and deployment of autonomous systems. They should specify rules for things such as transparency, accountability, fairness, and respect for human rights. As society and its mores change, so should the rules. Policymakers, developers and ethicists need to collaborate to come up with them.

- **Promoting Public Engagement** - First, the public must be actively engaged in talks about autonomous systems, to help build trust and ensure that their implementation stays on track with society's desires. By engaging with the public, through public consultations, school programmes and participatory approaches, we present an opportunity for more power and innovation in politics. People will be educated on the advantages and disadvantages of autonomous systems, which they can then seek to halt or encourage. When elites lose power, the political system will become far more representative.

- **Fostering Collaboration and Innovation -** Teamwork: progress demands close cooperation between public authorities, industry, academia and civil society. Public-private partnerships can help to share knowledge, resources and best practices, and facilitate joint decision-making; putting autonomous systems to work in the service of all types of people.

- **Investing in Research and Development** – An investment in research and development is needed to innovate autonomous capabilities and to overcome current challenges, such as ethical AI research, safety protocols, and privacy-preserving technologies. Governments and industry should fund and encourage this research into responsible and cutting-edge autonomous systems.

Future Directions

- **Advancing Autonomous AI Research** - Research into autonomous AI must continue to ADD new features and improvements to the capabilities of autonomous systems. More complex algorithms, more advanced sensors, decision making algorithms that allow for better levels of adaptation to a wider range of circumstances and challenges. They work together on a shared project to produce the best D designs. Collaborative research will continue to steer progress in the field.

- **Integrating Autonomous Systems with Emerging Technologies** - Taking advantage of emergent technologies like 5G communications, blockchain and quantum computing can give autonomous systems the tools to improve. For example, tools like blockchain can allow autonomous systems to store secure and verifiable data. Meanwhile, better communications networks such as 5G can accelerate the speed and reliability of decisions and execution, where needed.

- **Exploring Human-Autonomous System Collaboration -** Enhanced human-to-machine collaboration: New business, quality of life and social opportunities — and efficiencies — could emerge as we develop human-machine interfaces to increase seamless interaction, design training for 'the new worker' and deal with human-autonomous system 'teams'.

- **Ensuring Inclusive and Equitable Access** - Avoiding a digital divide, ensuring affordable access to autonomous systems, and establishing policy frameworks for inclusive development are key to building social equity. This ensures that autonomous systems are not closed off to the public but that the benefits they offer are accessible to everybody. 3. Enhancing quality of life across diversified populations is the goal.

Case Studies and Real-World Examples

- **Waymo: Autonomous Vehicles** - Waymo, a subsidiary of Alphabet Inc, is also a leader in AVs, with their own self-driving cars testing out on public roads for years now, accumulating millions of miles of real-world experience. As someone who loves cars and owns a few myself, I have fully embraced the self-driving technology. This is what makes the future exciting. If I'm in a rush, or just want a quiet ride, I can get into my driverless car and it will whisk me to my destination, with me just controlling music volume and air-conditioning to my satisfaction.

- **Tesla: Autopilot and Full Self-Driving -** Tesla's Autopilot and Full Self-Driving (FSD) features represent the technological capability to generate semi-autonomous and fully autonomous driving performance using AI capabilities. In many ways, Tesla has been unique as a vehicle manufacturer to exhibit strong dedication to developing and deploying those features.

- **Da Vinci Surgical System: Autonomous Surgery** - The da Vinci Surgical System, manufactured by the company Intuitive Surgical, is the first widely deployed autonomous surgical robot system, enabling minimally invasive precision and dexterity for surgeons. The da Vinci's market success firmly illustrates the potential of autonomy in healthcare.

- **Kiva Systems: Autonomous Warehousing** – Kiva Systems,

long since acquired by Amazon (now its Amazon Robotics sub-sidiary) pioneered autonomous robots for warehousing, in which case orders arrive to move around a warehouse by themselves, retrieving inventory items and ultimately helping to fulfil orders. Kiva's autonomous systems turned e-commerce logistics more efficient and scalable dramatically.

Conclusion

Autonomous systems promise enormous transformations of many areas of human life, especially in transportation, manufacturing, healthcare and service industries. Such systems can make life more efficient, safe and productive, but they come with important ethical, regulatory, privacy and economic challenges. How best to develop and deploy autonomous systems, and stay aboveboard in the process, will require ethical frameworks, more public engagement and deliberation, collaboration and ongoing research and innovation.

Furthermore, we should be able to tackle these issues and develop measures to promote responsible use – enabling the potential of autonomy to bring about socially progressive and truly inclusive forms of civic improvement. Leveraging the power of Artificial Intelligence and autonomous systems in a transparent and ethical way throughout civil society and the public sector is an indispensable pathway to more equitable and prosperous forms of social development.

CHAPTER 14

Preparing for the AI Future: Education and Skills

Introduction

The rapid advancement of artificial intelligence (AI) is reshaping industries and job markets, creating a pressing need for education systems to adapt and prepare individuals for the future. As AI continues to evolve, the skills required to thrive in the job market are also changing. This chapter explores the critical role of education in equipping individuals with the skills needed for the AI-driven future, discussing the transformation of educational practices, the development of new curricula, and strategies for lifelong learning.

The Changing Landscape of Work

- **Automation and Job Displacement** - AI and automation are transforming the workforce by automating routine and repetitive tasks. While this increases efficiency and productivity, it also leads to job displacement in sectors such as manufacturing, retail, and administrative services. Workers in these sectors need to adapt to the changing job market by acquiring new skills.

- **Emerging Job Role** - The rise of AI is also creating new job roles in fields such as data science, machine learning, AI ethics, and cybersecurity. These roles require a combination of technical skills, domain expertise, and soft skills. Education systems must evolve to provide training in these emerging areas to meet the demands of the AI-driven economy.

- **Skills Gap** - The rapid pace of technological change has resulted in a skills gap, where the skills possessed by the workforce do not match the skills required by employers. Addressing this gap is crucial for ensuring that individuals can access new job opportunities and that businesses can find the talent they need to innovate and grow.

Transforming Educational Practices

- **Personalized Learning** - AI-powered personalized learning platforms can tailor educational content to individual students' needs, preferences, and learning styles. These platforms use data analytics to assess students' strengths and weaknesses, providing customized learning paths and real-time feedback. Personalized learning enhances student engagement and improves learning outcomes.

- **Project-Based Learning** - Project-based learning (PBL) emphasizes hands-on, real-world projects that develop critical thinking, problem-solving, and collaboration skills. PBL encourages students to apply their knowledge to practical challenges, fostering creativity and innovation. Integrating AI projects into PBL can help students understand AI concepts and their applications.

- **Blended Learning** - Blended learning combines traditional classroom instruction with online learning, providing flexibility and access to a broader range of resources. AI-powered platforms can support blended learning by offering interactive content, virtual labs, and collaborative tools. This approach allows students to learn at their own pace while benefiting from in-person guidance and support.

- **Continuous Assessment and Feedback** - AI can enhance assessment practices by providing continuous and formative feedback to students. AI-driven tools can analyse student performance, identify areas for improvement, and offer personalized recommendations. Continuous assessment helps students stay on track and achieve their learning goals.

Developing New Curricula

- **AI Literacy** - AI literacy is essential for preparing individuals to understand and engage with AI technologies. AI literacy curricula should cover basic AI concepts, ethical considerations, and the impact of AI on society. Educators can use interactive tools, simulations, and case studies to teach AI literacy in an engaging and accessible manner.

- **STEM Education** - Science, technology, engineering, and mathematics (STEM) education is critical for developing the technical skills required for AI-related fields. Integrating AI and machine learning topics into STEM curricula can help students build a strong foundation in these areas. Hands-on projects, coding exercises, and interdisciplinary learning can enhance STEM education.

- **Soft Skills Development** - Soft skills, such as critical thinking, communication, collaboration, and emotional intelligence, are increasingly important in the AI-driven job market. Education systems should focus on developing these skills through group activities, discussions, and experiential learning. AI can support soft skills development by providing personalized feedback and facilitating virtual collaboration.

- **Ethics and Social Responsibility** - Understanding the ethical implications of AI is crucial for responsible AI development and deployment. Ethics curricula should cover topics such as bias, privacy, accountability, and the societal impact of AI. Engaging students in discussions, debates, and ethical dilemmas can help them develop a nuanced understanding of these issues.

Lifelong Learning and Reskilling

- **Lifelong Learning Culture** - Promoting a culture of lifelong learning is essential for individuals to adapt to the rapidly changing job market. Lifelong learning involves continuous skill development, professional growth, and personal enrichment. Encouraging individuals to pursue learning opportunities throughout their careers can help them stay relevant and resilient in the face of change.

- **Online Learning Platforms** - Online learning platforms, such as Coursera, edX, and Udacity, offer a wide range of courses and programs that can support lifelong learning and reskilling. These platforms provide flexible and accessible learning options for individuals seeking to acquire new skills or advance their careers. AI-driven personalization and adaptive learning enhance the effectiveness of online learning.

- **Corporate Training and Development** - Companies play a crucial role in supporting lifelong learning and reskilling through training and development programs. AI-powered learning management systems (LMS) can deliver personalized training, track employee progress, and identify skill gaps. Investing in employee development helps companies stay competitive and supports workforce retention and growth.

- **Public-Private Partnerships** - Public-private partnerships can facilitate lifelong learning and reskilling initiatives by leveraging the resources and expertise of both sectors. Collaborative programs can provide training opportunities, internships, and mentorship for individuals seeking to enter or transition within the job market. These partnerships can also support research and innovation in education and workforce development.

Strategies for Implementing AI Education

- **Investing in Educator Training** - Educators play a critical role in preparing students for the AI-driven future. Providing training and professional development opportunities for educators is essential to equip them with the knowledge and skills needed to teach AI-related subjects. Workshops, certification programs, and collaborative networks can support educators in integrating AI into their teaching practices.

- **Building Infrastructure and Resources** - Developing the necessary infrastructure and resources to support AI education is crucial. This includes providing access to technology, high-speed internet, and educational software. Schools and institutions should invest in creating AI labs, makerspaces, and collaborative learning environments to facilitate hands-on learning and experimentation.

- **Encouraging Industry Collaboration** - Collaboration between educational institutions and industry can enhance AI education by providing real-world insights, resources, and opportunities for students. Industry partnerships can support internships, apprenticeships, and project-based learning experiences. Engaging industry professionals as guest speakers, mentors, and advisors can enrich the learning experience.

- **Promoting Inclusive Access** - Ensuring inclusive access to AI education is essential to prevent widening disparities. Programs and initiatives should focus on reaching underserved communities, providing scholarships, and supporting diverse participation in AI-related fields. Addressing the digital divide and promoting equitable access to technology and resources are critical components of inclusive AI education.

Case Studies and Real-World Examples

- **Finland's AI Education Initiative** - Finland has launched an ambitious AI education initiative, including the "Elements of AI" online course, designed to teach the basics of AI to citizens. This initiative aims to democratize AI knowledge and ensure that the population is well-prepared for the AI-driven future. The course has been widely successful, attracting learners from diverse backgrounds.

- **AI 4 All: Promoting Diversity in AI** - AI 4 All is a nonprofit organization focused on increasing diversity and inclusion in AI education. The organization runs summer programs, workshops, and mentorship initiatives for underrepresented high school students. AI4All's programs aim to inspire the next generation of AI leaders and ensure that diverse perspectives are represented in AI development.

- **IBM's P-TECH Program** - IBM's P-TECH (Pathways in Technology Early College High Schools) program combines high school, college, and industry training to provide students with the skills needed for technology careers. The program integrates AI and STEM education, offering students hands-on learning experiences, internships, and mentorship opportunities. P-TECH graduates earn both a high school diploma and an associate degree.

- **Google's AI for Social Go** - Google's AI for Social Good initiative supports projects that use AI to address social and environmental challenges. The initiative provides funding, resources, and mentorship for researchers and organizations working on AI-driven solutions. By promoting AI for social good, Google aims to ensure that AI benefits all members of society.

Future Directions

- **Integrating AI in Early Education** - Integrating AI concepts and tools in early education can spark interest and build foundational skills from a young age. Introducing coding, robotics, and AI-related activities in primary and secondary schools can inspire students and prepare them for advanced studies. Early exposure to AI fosters curiosity and a growth mindset.

- **Expanding Interdisciplinary Learning** - Expanding interdisciplinary learning involves integrating AI education with other subjects, such as humanities, social sciences, and arts. This approach helps students understand the broader implications of AI and develop a well-rounded perspective. Interdisciplinary projects and collaborations can foster creativity and critical thinking.

- **Fostering Global Collaboration** - Fostering global collaboration in AI education involves sharing best practices, resources, and expertise across borders. International partnerships can support the development of global standards and curricula for AI education. Collaborative initiatives can address global challenges and promote equitable access to AI.

- **Emphasizing Ethical AI Development** - Emphasizing ethical AI development in education ensures that future AI practitioners are mindful of the ethical implications of their work. This includes teaching students about bias, fairness, transparency, and accountability. Ethical AI education fosters a culture of responsibility and social impact.

Preparing for the AI future requires a transformative approach to education and skills development. As AI reshapes industries and job markets, education systems must evolve to equip individuals with the knowledge, skills, and mindset needed to thrive

This involves personalized learning, project-based learning, and continuous assessment, as well as developing new curricula that emphasize AI literacy, STEM education, soft skills, and ethics.

Lifelong learning and reskilling are essential to ensure that individuals can adapt to the changing job market and seize new opportunities. Strategies such as investing in educator training, building infrastructure, encouraging industry collaboration, and promoting inclusive access are critical for implementing AI education effectively.

By addressing these challenges and embracing these strategies, we can prepare individuals for the AI-driven future, fostering innovation, resilience, and social equity. As we move forward, it is imperative to prioritize ethical considerations, interdisciplinary learning, and global collaboration to ensure that AI education promotes a just and prosperous society for all.

Conclusion

This chapter explored the seismic shifts that the world of work is undergoing due to AI and the role that education will play in meeting this challenge. As AI matures, it not only transforms jobs, automating away those tasks that it is able to carry out reliably, but also spawns new jobs and postings that require an even deeper blend of technical and soft skills. Bridging the skills gap in this way will be vital in ensuring that the world of work is not left struggling in the Information Age.

Adapting practices in education is at the heart of this adaptation. Personalised learning based on AI-powered learning enhances belief among students because these AI powered platforms provide enhanced learning experiences based on each learner's specific learning style and needs, which in turn leads to greater engagement and outcomes. The increasing emphasis on project-based learning (PBL), where learners learn to think and solve problems, will flourish. Additionally, blended learning that takes place in both classroom and online environments provides flexibility and a larger resource base for students. AI tools that provide continuous assessment offer the opportunity of providing learners with real-time feedback to keep them on track with their learning goals.

It's equally critical to develop new curricula to help individuals navigate these changes. A focus on AI literacy, STEM education, soft skills and ethical development must be core elements of an educational roadmap that prepares individuals to help shape the use of AI technologies and support the responsible development and deployment of AI.

There is a legitimate need to reskill the workforce to adapt to the challenges presented by an AI-driven job market, and to ensure a culture of ongoing learning for life. On-line learning platforms are playing a key role in offering flexible and affordable opportunities for education. Corporate training programs and public-private partnerships are supporting the reskilling efforts of individuals and companies.

It also requires purposeful investments in educator preparedness, infrastructure, industry partnerships, and whether it's accessible to all. We now point to the Finland example of AI education. We refer to programmes such as AI4All, an AI education initiative funded by contributions of over $125 million from industry and governments across Finland. We point to IBM's P-TECH programme for wider access to higher education in science and technology (with a particular emphasis on AI), and Google's AI for Social Good programme focused on addressing challenges in healthcare, education and the environment.

Moving forward, efforts to incorporate notions of AI in early education, making interdisciplinary learning more of the norm, encouraging international collaboration, and enriching the focus on ethical AI development are essential. In so doing, we will help develop the thinking skills, innovation and flexibility, and an understanding of social equity that people will need to thrive in an AI future-ready world. Placing ethics and a global focus at the forefront of AI education ensures that this education is aimed at sustaining and creating a just and equitable world for all.

CHAPTER 15

AI in the Arts and Creativity: Redefining Human Expression

Introduction

Artificial intelligence (AI) is transforming the arts and creativity in many exciting ways. It represents a set of tools and mediums that allow artists to be more creative and communicate in new ways. Going forward, music and visual arts, novels and poetry, film and interactive gaming will all be transformed by human artists working with machine intelligence and creativity. This chapter will examine the transformative impact of AI in the arts, survey applications and benefits, highlight some of the remaining challenges, and consider the future of AI in creative expression. By studying the synergy between AI and the arts, we can gain new appreciation for how technology is changing the way humans express themselves through art and extend the capacity of the human imagination.

AI in Music

- **Composition and Production -** AI-powered voice-to-sheet music and voice-to-audio orchestration systems are now possible. AI algorithms could well automatically create melodies, harmonies and rhythms from scratch. This creates interesting forms of 'composition by collaboration': composers could play with AI tools such as Muse Net by OpenAI and Amper Music. Additionally, we can imagine algorithms helping us to produce music, from mixing and mastering to sound design. This could take production tasks to the next level in terms of efficiency and quality.

- **Personalized Music Recommendations** - Streaming services such as Spotify or Apple Music, for example, use machine learning algorithms to make context-based recommendations to its users about what they might want to listen to. Drawing on what genre or tempo of music you have listened to, as well as how much or for how long, algorithms can suggest music that reflects your listening preferences. The benefit of these personalised recommendations is that they provide the listener with music that they wouldn't have found themselves (that is, without being 'told' what to listen to next).

- **Interactive Music Experiences** - interactive music experiences that require three-way engagement between listener, musician/ music, and AI (5 words) For example, AI instruments that generate music in real time, responsive to explicit or implicit user-provided inputs or external factors. Interactive AI-powered installations and performances could detect and respond to audience interactions. Forms of music creation and consumption previously not possible or practical may now become accessible in imaginative new contexts and configurations.

AI in Visual Arts

- **Generative Art** - Generative art, for example, taps into AI algorithms to generate visual artworks. Techniques such as Generative Adversarial Networks (GANs) or neural style transfer allow for the automated generation of visuals that are at the same time original and highly nuanced, and where artists such as the German digital artist Mario Klingemann or the young Turkish artist Rafik Anadolu are setting tracks. These imaginative creative endeavours are forcing us to think differently about what constitutes creativity and authorship.

- **Augmented Creativity** - AI enhances the creative process of human artists by offering new skills and understandings. Mashups like Deep Art or Artbreeder can give artists a sense of how visual features in different styles or colour schemes might be combined and allow them to produce new ideas and inspirations. AI can also analyse existing artworks to uncover patterns and suggest improvements to support artists in refining their art.

- **AI-Curated Exhibitions** - AI has already been deployed to curate art exhibitions by examining and clustering large databases of works. By identifying thematic linkages, histories and aesthetic correspondences, AI-supported curators can propose exhibitions that speak to one another across different time-periods and contexts, providing new perspectives and continuities in art history and contemporary practice. AI-curated exhibitions enrich our reading of artworks and, ultimately, our experience as their viewers.

AI in Literature and Writing

- **Automated Writing and Storytelling** - AI is both altering how literature is written today and enhancing writing's prospects. Thanks to powerful AI models such as GPT-3, and a wealth of online training data, it's now possible to automatically generate almost any type of text, from poetry and short stories, to essays and articles. AI can help writers in a collaborative fashion, allowing them to experiment with new types of narrative structures and styles.AI-powered 'writing tools' are also being applied to content creation for marketing, journalism and entertainment.

- **Interactive Fiction and Games** - The more AI is integrated with interactive fiction and gaming, the more dynamic the narratives will become, responding to player choices at every turn of a game. For example, AI game engines give rise to adaptive storylines, dialogue and scenarios based on a player's actions to enhance personalisation. In 'generate-on-demand' interactive fiction platforms such as AI Dungeon, the user feeds in fictional content and, together with the AI, the user becomes a co-creator, immersing into participatory narratives.

- **Text Analysis and Insights** - AI text analysis tools help authors and researchers better understand word patterns, themes and sentiment in written work. Such technology enables the detection of trends across mass quantities of text, while enhancing readability and refining these writing samples along the way, which can then improve quality and overall appeal. Grammarly and Pro Writing Aid are examples of strategies taken to this effect, which use AI to monitor feedback as a work-in-progress is developed and composed.

AI in Film and Animation

- **Scriptwriting and Storyboarding** - Artificial intelligence (AI) helps to create scripts and storyboards for animated feature films and TV shows. This includes AI-generated plot concepts, character descriptions and dialogues, and applications that produce storyboards. The AI tools create AI-based plots, storyboarding versions of film or TV scripts and applying statistical analysis to adjust visual sequences, such as shot order, duration and placement. This application streamlines the pre-production process, making it more creative and productive.

- **Visual Effects and Animation** - AI is now making powerful inroads into the world of visual effects (VFX) and animation by automating many of the tasks, such as motion capture, character animation and rendering, that used to require human grunt work. AI can now be used to simulate just about any behaviour or natural phenomenon such as water, fire or smoke, halving shoot times and dramatically reducing costs. AI can also now be used to engineer animation tools such as Dee Motion and Adobe Character Animator that artists can use to make their onscreen characters appear more real.

- **Content Personalization and Recommendation** - Film and animation content is suggested to viewers to cater to their interests and previous engagements. Platforms such as Netflix and YouTube recommend individual movies and shows to their users using machine learning and algorithms. Personalised film and animation recommendations can greatly enhance the experience for viewers, and aid content creators towards their target audience.

Benefits of AI in the Arts

- **Enhanced Creativity and Innovation** – AI enables creativity and innovation by giving artists new material and tools for their art. For instance, through apps driven by AI, human creators can mix, match, emulate and reimagine styles, formats, and the very dynamic of an artform itself. The invention of original works can be the result of the merge of human creativity and machine intelligence.

- **Increased Accessibility and Participation** - AI democratises the tools and resources of artmaking, allowing more people to do more creative activities. AI-based platforms level the playing field for artistic production, making music, visual arts, writing and animation more accessible and affordable. The more options that are easy and open to more people, the richer – and more diverse – the creative community will be.

- **Efficient Production and Distribution** - Through automating repetitive and time-consuming processes from production to distribution, AI enables artworks that once required days, months, or even years of repetitive labour to be produced in a matter of minutes or hours. AI also enables artists to concentrate on the creative part of the work while letting algorithms take care of the editing, rendering or marketing of the artworks. AI-driven platforms enable the distribution of artworks to global audiences and create visibility in ways that were previously not possible.

Challenges and Ethical Considerations

1. **Authenticity and Originality** - In relation to the arts, the use of AI poses questions about authorship and originality: if a piece of art is created by an AI or with its help, it becomes hard to determine the author and the degree of creativity of the final artefact. Public knowledge of the role that the AI played in the creation process is central in helping to solve these challenges and retain the purity of the creative process.

2. **Bias and Representation** - Given that AI algorithms tend to reproduce the biases of the historical data that they're trained on, the resulting representations that we ultimately create

through deep learning could end up reflecting any pre-existing biases in the dataset. In both cases, art generated by AI could perpetuate stereotypes and fail to provide the same countercultural or diverse viewpoints that famous human artists like Mizuki have historically provided. It may seem counterintuitive, or even politically correct, to be concerned about fairness when it comes to algorithmically produced art. But producing art with unique and idiosyncratic artistic styles that challenge old stereotypes and perspectives – such as those produced by microrod, Midjourney or Stable Diffusion – is a fundamentally important artistic goal, as is targeting a diverse array of users. For example, studies suggest that females and nonbinary people tend to be underrepresented in AI research. To address these concerns, we should be careful to develop and train AI models on datasets that are as diverse and representative as possible.

3. **Intellectual Property and Copyright** - There is also considerable ambiguity at the nexus of AI and intellectual property, where concerns about copyright and ownership abound. Consensus is needed on who gets the rights to AI-generated artworks – the artist, or the AI developer? How do we ensure that the rights of artists and creators are protected in the mainstreaming of AI in the arts?

4. **Ethical Use of AI** - First, ethical uses of AI in the arts must respect and benefit artists and audiences and promote access while respecting the values and practices of the artistic and cultural community. They must generate artistic work in ways that do not jeopardise but rather foster the dignity and capa-

bilities of human agents and audiences and must aim at generating valuable cultural and social outputs (both artistically and as a means of expression). The implementation of an ethics for data-driven artistic practices must also focus on generative questions: how to guarantee fair representation when AI is used, and ensure such representation respects diversity, difference and equality. When it comes to new and experimental art methodologies, such questions give rise to others. While an ethics for data-driven arts creates the promise of breaking artistic boundaries and expanding creativity, we should also think in terms of what these methodologies cannot or should not do. A machine is only as creative as the humans who program it to be so. Along these lines, ethical uses of AI must be able to both select and prohibit creations. It is not enough to restrict malicious use of technology, for example using it to produce non-consensual pornography.

Future Directions

- **Human-AI Collaboration** - The future of AI in the arts lies in this collaborative space with users, and humans will continue exploring how to create new forms of collaboration with assistance from AI – AI as a creative partner, as a creative force, which inspires the human imagination and augments that human creativity, and learning to recognise what kind of thinking new bits of intelligence can bring to our own.

- **Interdisciplinary Approaches** - Drawing on the arts, AI and related disciplines such as neuroscience, psychology and cultural studies might help to develop better forms of orally based creativity, discern aesthetic values, and build new artistic competencies. - Interdisciplinary approaches can help to understand the cognitive and emotional underpinnings of creativity and create more humanlike AI.

- **AI-Enhanced Art Education** - And by including AI in the curriculums of art education for the next generation of artists, students can be prepared for the AI future that lies ahead of us. AI assisted tutorials and creative programs on the web can help art education reach all corners of the world by providing personalised artefacts and tutorials on demand, and more practice scenarios, and more intricated problems for them to be creative with. 5AI can help encourage digital literacy and creative thinking by using AI-powered tools in curriculums for the next generation, to make them learn, think and be creative, instead of feeling vulnerable and threatened.

- **Expanding the Boundaries of Art** - Think of AI as an especially powerful artistic medium of expression – one that allows us to expand the concept of art by creating new types of experiences or by introducing meaningful multisensory art, private or public art installations, virtual or augmented reality, AI-driven live theatre performances, and more. In doing so, new artistic genres and types of artistic practices might emerge.

Case Studies and Real-World Examples

- **OpenAI's Muse Net** - The constructivist story is exemplified by the OpenAI model from 2021, Muse Net. Muse Net is a music generation model that can compose music in multiple styles and genres as diverse as baroque or impressionist while also integrating new textures and elements from other genres, demonstrating the tech's ability to inspire the creation of entirely novel musical schemes or collaborations.

- **Deep Art** – Deep Art is an app to transform photos into new images using the neural networks of famous artists. Its users can upload pictures and apply artistic filters to recreate visual styles. Deep Art gives a glimpse of how AI might democratise tools and methods, and how it can allow for more creative experimentation.

- **GPT-3 and Interactive Fiction** - The AI language model GPT-3 by OpenAI generates dynamic narratives for interactive fiction tools such as AI Dungeon as directed by user inputs, including its own storylines and character responses, proving itself capable of recognition and coherent illustration of plot, thematic development, occasional witty remarks, and more. AI could enable more diverse, compelling and nuanced narratives than humans currently create.

- **Refik Anadol's AI Art** – **Refik Anadol** is a leader in using AI to create large-scale data-driven art installations and paintings, which explore the boundaries of art, science and technology. He has produced projects such as 'Melting Memories' and his newly launched 'Machine Hallucination'.

Conclusion

AI is poised to overhaul the arts and creativity as well, by offering new tools, new media and new ways to discover new possibilities. Art is being generated by AI systems, and fundamentally rethought; it is being produced and viewed in whole new ways, and AI can help us better understand this art – as it can artforms of all kinds. The explosion in AI-derived art, across disciplines including music, sound, visual arts, literature and film, presents a uniquely complex set of choices and challenges in accepting and understanding the role of AI in our art and culture. The rise of AI carries the promise of new modes, methods and mediums to generate and make art, but it's crucial to confront the doubts and trepidations about judgments on authenticity, bias, rights, legacy and intellect. These persistent problems must be addressed if we're to ensure the safe and equitable use of this technology.

Further, it emphasises three future directions: human-AI collaboration, interdisciplinarity, and AI applications in art education & training. Lastly, the conclusion highlights the importance of addressing ethical concerns in fashioning AI for the arts and stresses that the possibilities and limitations of AI in the arts remain to be explored. In sum, we can use the advantages of AI in the arts and fashion a diverse and vibrant future for the arts by exploring new hybrid forms, encouraging cross-disciplinary approaches, nurturing collaborative human-AI endeavours and igniting experimental endeavours to explore the boundaries of artistic expression, all while addressing ethical concerns.

Looking to the future, we should stop comparing the two and acknowledge each of them on its own terms, focusing on what human and machine creativity bring to the art of collaboration. With moral and considered use, AI has the power to pave the way to a culture where technology helps rather than hinders the creation of a more diverse and multifaceted creative world.

CHAPTER 16

*AI and Environmental Sustainability:
A Path to a Greener Future*

Introduction

Environmental sustainability has become one of the key areas of research and realisation in recent times that has led to the increasing use of artificial intelligence (AI) for envisioning solutions to the ecological concerns. AI can be a game-changer in the way we manage our natural resources and combat climate change, sustainability issues due to pollution and any other ill effects on the environment. In this chapter, we will delve deeper into the significance of AI in environmental sustainability, its domain use, benefits and challenges along with its potential future directions. Leveraging AI can help us usher in a greener world and bring wellness to our planet and its future generations.

AI in Climate Change Mitigation

- **Climate Modelling and Prediction -** AI improves climate modelling and prediction by sifting through and making sense of massive amounts of data from a wide range of sources, such as satellite imagery, weather stations and historic climate records. Machine learning algorithms can identify patterns and make better predictions about the course of changing climates and the occurrence of extreme weather events. These insights help decision-makers and researchers improve how they adapt to and mitigate the effects of climate change.

- **Carbon Emission Reduction** - AI technologies can maximise energy efficiency and emissions-reductions in a wide range of sectors. For example, AI-based energy management systems continuously monitor energy flows via sensors and actuators and adjust energy usage accordingly to optimise performance while decreasing emissions. We've also witnessed AI-based systems revamping data-centre energy use at companies such as Google and Microsoft, as they compete to lower the carbon footprint of massive computing operations.

- **Renewable Energy Integration** - AI can help to integrate renewable energy into the power grid. For example, AI algorithms can help to forecast energy production from solar, wind and hydro sources to ensure supply and demand match. AI systems can also help to optimise the operation of renewable energy plants, delivering vital energy as efficiently and reliably as possible. What all this means is that AI can encourage the transition to renewable energy sources, playing an important role in delivering a sustainable energy future.

AI in Resource Management

- **Water Resource Management** - AI technologies are changing the way water resources are managed through improved water usage, leak detection and demand forecasting. By analysing data from sensors and meters, AI-based systems with a clear understanding of physical locations can track the distribution of water in a network in real time, sending alerts and creating a picture of the most efficient and cost-effective ways of using water. AI systems can also analyse many times more data from various sources, reducing errors and making smarter decisions about using irrigation systems in agriculture.

- **Agricultural Sustainability** - AI is also making agriculture smarter by giving farmers timely and data-based insights and recommendations. With the help of AI, operational techniques that are based on precision agriculture are leading to the optimisation of crop yields, the use of fewer pesticides and fertilisers, as well as natural resource conservation. The AI-powered Farm Logs and Climate Field View platforms examine the soil health, weather and crop conditions to provide farmers with suggestions and make agriculture more eco-friendly.

- **Waste Management and Recycling** - AI can improve the sorting of recycling materials and timings of waste-collections, allowing fast and accurate separation of recyclable materials. Artificial intelligence (AI) enables automated and accurate separation of different kinds of waste, for instance by means of robots and sensors, that far exceeds manual sorting methods. Such sorting can improve the recycling rate and decrease waste. Thanks to AI, the transition to a circular economy appears feasible.

AI in Biodiversity and Conservation

- **Wildlife Monitoring and Protection** - Wildlife populations are now monitored and safeguarded from poachers by artificial-intelligence technologies. AI-based cameras and drones are now tracking animal movements, detecting poaching activity and monitoring habitats remotely in real time, while image and sound features can be distinguished by machine-learning algorithms to identify species and determine their wellbeing. Consequently, conservationists are now able to perform predictive actions to preserve threatened species and biodiversity.

- **Habitat Restoration** - AI helps habitat restoration by processing environmental data and predicting the success of restoration projects. AI-backed models can detect degraded landscapes and recommend plant species for reforestation and afforestation, while monitoring and optimising restoration activities. Thanks to its use in habitat restoration, AI helps building back the environment and improving biodiversity.

- **Marine Conservation** - AI is being used in marine conservation to monitor wellbeing and health of the ocean, track marine species and illegally caught fish, and identify illegal fishing activities. Self-propelled autonomous underwater vehicles (AUVs) equipped with microprocessors and computer vision cameras can collect vast amounts of data on water quality parameters, health of coral reefs and marine life, and analyse that data using machine learning algorithms to support protected areas management for conservation and sustainable fisheries. AI can measure temperature.

Benefits of AI in Environmental Sustainability

- **Enhanced Decision-Making** - AI can provide the data-based information in real time that policymakers, businesses and other environmentalists need to make better decisions to promote sustainability. AI analysis tools can flag trends, outcomes and improvements that can extend the life of resources and reduce environmental impact overall.

- **Efficiency and Cost Savings** – AI makes everything greener by helping to optimise resource use and cut costs. AI-driven systems can be designed to maximise efficiency and lower production costs, especially in industries such as agriculture, energy and waste management. For example, water is increasingly being seen as a crucial resource for the future. In some parts of the world, millions of people live without proper access to clean drinking water. Some companies – such as mine – are trialling AI systems to help make agriculture more efficient and even grow new sources of food supply. AI can control water use in crops better, maximising the crop yield and minimising water being wasted. And at an industrial level, AI solutions can also help reduce water loss across the entire food supply chain. This could become crucial in the future, when water scarcity and the related cost implications could have significant impacts on our agricultural system. Overall, we enjoy various benefits thanks to the great disruptive promise of AI.

- **Scalability and Impact** - AI can help us tackle environmental issues at a planetary scale. Since AI can be brought to scale, it can be deployed across jurisdictions and sectors on a massive scale, and it assures that merely repetitive tasks can be automated. These solutions can then be scaled up without any impedance in terms of deployment across different affected geographies. That means, if a particular solution to an environmental problem is successful in one part of the world it can be easily replicated in all the other parts.

Challenges and Ethical Considerations

1. **Data Privacy and Security** - The use of AI for environmental sustainability can involve the collection of large amounts of data. It is necessary to ensure that this data is protected to prevent unauthorised access to sensitive information, minimise the risk of

hacking, and maintain public trust. Privacy and security in digital ecosystems call for robust data protection and compliance with protection regulation.

2. **Bias and Fairness** – As AI algorithms take what's been called the 'garbage in, garbage out' principle to a whole new level, they will also inherit biases from the data they're trained on and offer biased outcomes in environmental management. This means that environmental managers should use multi-layered representative ethical datasets to train their models, and also regularly audit their models to check for bias. We must boost fairness in AI-driven environmental solutions so as to avoid disrupting ecosystems and marginalised communities.

3. **Ethical Use of AI -** In the case of the ethical use of AI for environmental sustainability purposes, considerations need to be addressed concerning whether the impacts of the AI action on ecosystems and communities will be positive or negative and whether those impacts will last in the long term. Authors' words: To assess the risk/benefit and evaluate the fit of the AI solutions with ethical values and sustainability targets, trust and legitimacy (i.e., transparent and accountable AI culture and practices) should be enhanced at the early stages of AI design.

4. **Access and Inclusivity** - Distributing resources for AI consumption and solutions to increase environmental sustainability for people and places who might be underserved and in need. Promoting AI that's more diverse, inclusive, and equitable will help share AI advantages while developing AI technologies and solutions to benefit the environment – and everyone.

Future Directions

- **AI for Circular Economy -** While there are many ways AI can be used to support the circular economy, here are some key examples: At the design stage, AI can be used to optimise the use of resources in products and find ways to increase resource recovery or maximise recycling and reuse. At the operations stage, AI can be used in systems to manage the circular use of products, and to trigger corrective choices for repair, reuse or recycling of end-of-life products. At the consumption stage, AI can be used in systems to support consumers in their everyday use of products, anticipating the need to repair or consider charging, networking or repair options before an end-of-life situation arises.AI also has the potential to enable a more sustainable industry through reduced environmental impact.

- **AI and Renewable Energy Innovations -** AI use in environmental sustainability will foster innovations in renewable-energy technologies. Artificial intelligence can help to improve the efficiency of solar panels, wind turbines and energy storage, to make renewable energy sources more competitive and reliable. AI could facilitate the search for new renewable-energy technologies and materials, to help bring that energy future online.

- **Collaborative AI for Global Environmental Challenges** – international collaboration and deploying AI across both sectors and regions: International collaboration, public-private partnerships and trans disciplinarity can leverage AI to tackle global environmental problems such as climate change, loss of biodiversity, depletion of resources and many others. Collaborative AI can enable generating synergies between sectors and regions and pooling resources, knowledge and scale.

- **AI for Climate Resilience** – AI can bolster climate resilience: Climate change is upending communities and ecosystems worldwide, and here AI can help. Models can gauge vulnerabilities and predict extreme weather events and recommend adaptive steps that can enhance resilience. If AI is integrated into climate resilience planning, mitigation efforts and responses to predicted climate changes will be more informed.

Case Studies and Real-World Examples

- **Google's Project Sunroof** - Google's Project Sunroof employs AI to analyse satellite photographs and calculate a building's available solar potential. The tool enables homeowners to determine how much they might save in utility costs and how much carbon would be avoided if they switched to solar, and to receive costs from local installers. Project Sunroof reveals the potential for AI to accelerate the uptake of renewable energy once individuals have the relevant information presented in actionable ways.

- **Microsoft's AI for Earth** - Microsoft started an AI for Earth initiative that funds projects using AI to work on climate change, biodiversity loss and scarce water, providing funding, tools and technical support so that researchers and organisations can utilise AI for sustainable solutions. AI for Earth provides a starting point for how AI might be useful for and perhaps better, used in the sustainable future.

- **The Ocean Cleanup** - The Ocean Cleanup involves the use of AI-enabled drones and sensors for the detection and extraction of plastic waste from the world's oceans and waterways. Using AI, debris can be detected, collection monitored, and cleanup can be automated to optimise its efficiency. Ocean Cleanup's large-scale application of AI shows that the protection of ocean ecosystems can coincide with technological innovation.

- **Agricultural AI Platforms** - For farmers in the field, there are apps such as Climate Field View and Farm Logs that use AI to track crop performance for farmers and encourage them to adapt best practices to reach their targets. Spider Takeaway-These applications use data to provide farmers with insights into artificial intelligence farming, such as when to sow seeds, how to optimise water usage or clarify what pests should be eliminated. These apps use data on soil health, weather patterns and crop conditions to help farmers identify problems and find appropriate solutions. By using this data, artificial intelligence farming aids in resource conservation and increases food security.

Conclusion

We argued that AI would be a game-changer for tackling environmental sustainability in solving challenges such as climate change mitigation, resource use and management, and biodiversity conservation. The opportunities lie in improved decision-making, efficiency, scalability and impact. However, much more needs to be done on data privacy, bias, appropriate application and equity.

Some potential areas where AI could bring further benefits in the fight for environmental sustainability include enhancing the circular economy, supporting the growth of renewable energies, fostering collaboration, and facilitating climate resilience. Application of AI can help craft effective plans for a green planet and a sustainable development.

As we move forward, making sure the ethical, equitable and collaborative approach leads the way as the technology is designed and applied is vital to ensure that we use AI to lead us to a greener future.

Charting the Future of AI

Artificial intelligence (AI) is an irreversible force that has already begun to transform our world. Whether harnessing algorithms to enhance healthcare, education, governance or sustainability, the rise of automated artificial intelligence is now integral to our planet-wide project of progress. However, before AI's project becomes the destiny of our planet, we must first turn a critical eye onto our past and plan for its future.

The Promise and Potential of AI

Across this book, we've journeyed through how AI can help transform industries, improve efficiencies and change our lives for the better. In healthcare, it provides diagnoses for early disease before life-changing outcomes can happen, and tailored treatment plans for those a bit further out. In education, it serves up individualised learning pathways and prepares the workforce for the challenges of the fourth industrial revolution. In governance, it helps improve decision making and build in transparency. AI has the capacity to process more data than ever before, spot patterns and then decide what to do with them. And that's just taking it apart block by block.

Balancing Innovation and Ethics

Yes, its usefulness is immense, but how we build and use AI systems ethically is hugely important. Biased AI algorithms will lead to unfair results; collecting data raises questions regarding individual privacy; and autonomous AI systems raise questions of moral responsibility. Ethical considerations of fairness, transparency and accountability must build into the mosaic. Because the rapid changes happening in AI may lead to decisions that work well for computers but deeply harm people. We must act not to kill the golden goose but to ensure that it flies in a flock of ethically cared-for birds.

The challenge of ethical AI is therefore not only a technological subject but also a societal challenge and will require the expertise and collaboration of not only technologists and ethicists but also policymakers and the wider public in developing AI systems that respect our values and ethics. In an era of accelerating innovation, we must ensure that the emerging AI technologies benefit all of humanity and foster the greater social good.

Preparing for an AI-Driven Future

Things happen fast in AI, so we need to be prepared, and that means teaching more (and more people) technical skills than ever – but also arming us all with the critical thinking, creativity and ethical reasoning that will help us cope with an AI-enabled future. We also need robust lifelong learning and reskilling in place so that people can respond to change. It is about learning how to learn, learning new things, and learning about ourselves.

Moreover, we need public involvement and engagement: people need to understand what AI can do, and what its implications are for our lives; so that they can have an informed influence on its development.

Promoting Inclusivity and Equity

AI could be instrumental in closing social divides but could also widen them if development and deployment aren't made more responsible. Keeping AI inclusive and equitable implies breaking down the digital divide, fostering greater participation by women and people of colour in AI-related industries and professions, and AIs that also consider humans on the margins.

Moreover, we need to build global solidarity. The problems and opportunities that AI presents are increasingly globalised in nature, calling for greater international collaboration. Sharing knowledge, resources and best practices between countries helps to ensure that the benefits of AI are more widely disseminated.

The Role of AI in Environmental Sustainability

Environmental sustainability is one of the biggest issues that we face today. AI can help us reduce climate change and its consequences, let us better manage our natural resources and help us develop sustainable behaviour. By taking full advantage of AI, we can take measures to preserve our Earth and secure a sustainable future for the next generations of humans.

Looking Ahead

We have a deep sense that AI will remain a source of invention and change into the future, with all the promise and peril that this entails.

How shall we proceed?

We are only at the dawn of artificial intelligence, and its course will be determined by how we fulfil the promises and surpass the challenges of the present. By building a culture that is accountable, generative and lifelong, we can enable AI to guide us toward a better, fairer, safer future – for itself and us.

The goal of this book has been to offer a truly multifaceted portrait of AI's effects, and to share some ideas about how we can manage them. Let's continue to have that conversation, keeping alive the traditions of ethical innovation. We're committed to doing our best to work together to chart a future where AI serves as a force for good in our society.

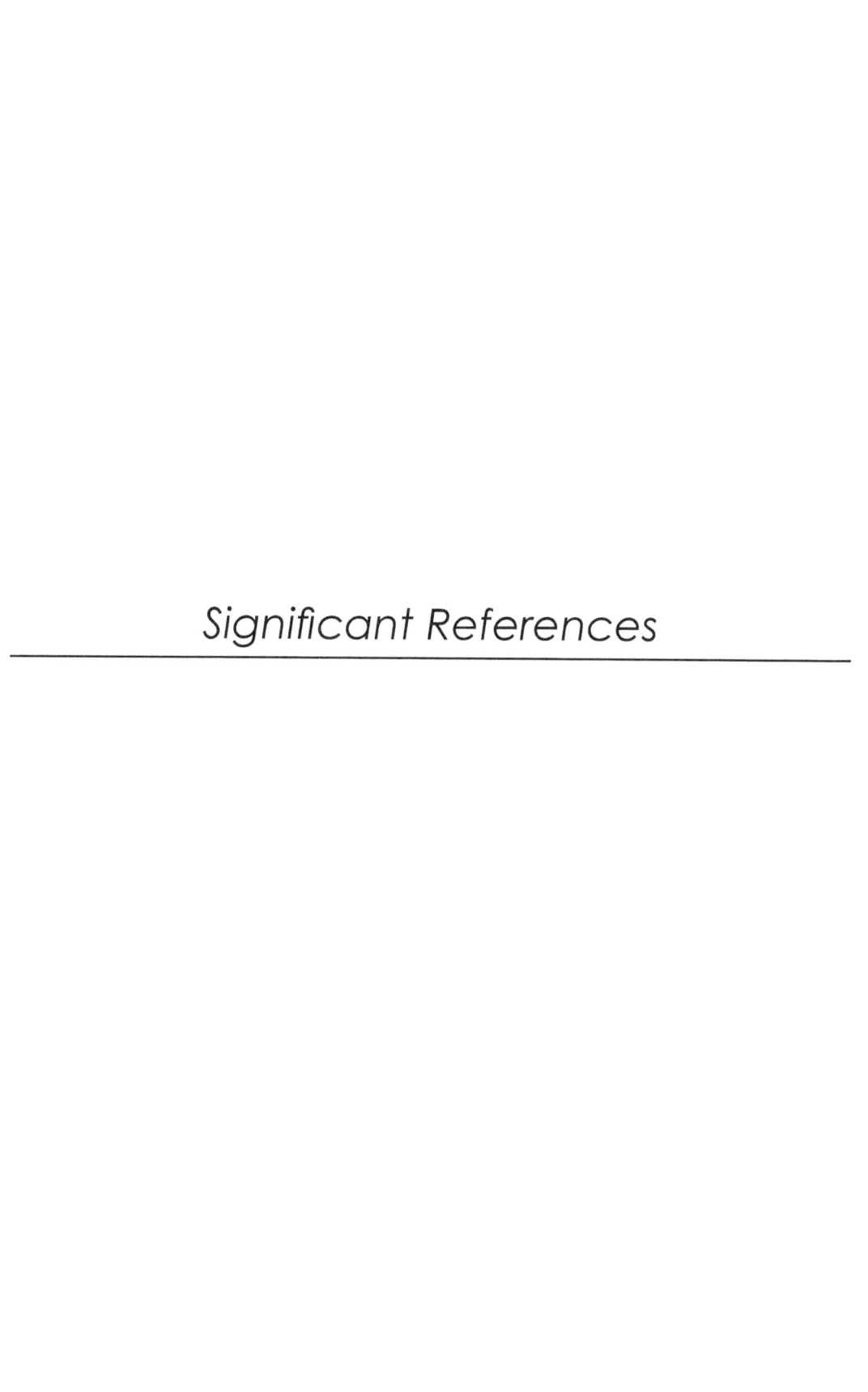

Significant References

1. Nick Bostrom, Superintelligence: Paths, Dangers, Strategies. Oxford University Press, 2014 - This seminal work explores the potential future scenarios involving superintelligent AI and the existential risks they pose to humanity. Bostrom discusses paths to achieve superintelligence and strategies to manage its impact, advocating for proactive measures to ensure safety and alignment with human values.

2. Stuart Russell and Peter Norvig, Artificial Intelligence: A Modern Approach Pearson, 2020 - This comprehensive textbook covers the breadth of AI, from basic principles to advanced topics. It is widely used in academic settings and provides a thorough grounding in AI methodologies, applications, and theoretical foundations.

3. Max Tegmark, Life 3.0: Being Human in the Age of Artificial Intelligence. Knopf, 2017 - Tegmark's book delves into the implications of AI on society and human life. He categorizes the evolution of life into three stages and focuses on the third stage, where AI could redefine what it means to be human. He explores potential futures and the ethical questions they raise.

4. Erik Brynjolfsson and Andrew McAfee, The Second Machine Age: Work, Progress, and Prosperity in a Time of Brilliant Technologies. W.W. Norton & Company, 2014 - This book discusses how digital technologies, including AI, are transforming the economy and society. The authors highlight the opportunities and challenges presented by these changes, emphasizing the need for adaptive strategies in the workforce and policy.

5. Cathy O'Neil, Weapons of Math Destruction: How Big Data Increases Inequality and Threatens Democracy. Crown, 2016 - O'Neil examines how algorithms and big data can perpetuate inequality and undermine democratic processes. She provides case studies of algorithmic bias and calls for greater accountability and transparency in the use of AI.

6. Pedro Domingos, The Master Algorithm: How the Quest for the Ultimate Learning Machine Will Remake Our World. Basic Books, 2015 - Domingos introduces the concept of a "master algorithm" that can learn anything from data. He explores different types of machine learning and their applications, offering insights into the future of AI and its transformative potential.

7. Calum Chace, Surviving AI: The Promise and Peril of Artificial Intelligence. Three Cs, 2015 - Chace discusses the dual aspects of AI—its potential benefits and the existential risks it poses. He provides a balanced view of how AI could affect different sectors and the importance of preparing for its widespread adoption.

8. Luciano Floridi, The Ethics of Information. Oxford University Press, 2013 - Floridi's work focuses on the ethical dimensions of information technology, including AI. He argues for a new ethical framework to address the unique challenges posed by digital technologies, emphasizing the need for responsible innovation.

9. Yuval Noah Harari, Homo Deus: A Brief History of Tomorrow. Harper, 2017 - Harari explores future trends and technologies, including AI, that could shape the next stage of human evolution. He discusses the potential for AI to augment human capabilities and the ethical dilemmas this raises.

10. Viktor Mayer-Schönberger and Kenneth Cukier, Big Data: A Revolution That Will Transform How We Live, Work, and Think. Houghton Mifflin Harcourt, 2013 - This book examines how big data analytics are transforming various sectors. The authors highlight the power of data-driven decision-making and the importance of managing data responsibly to avoid ethical pitfalls.

11. Andreas Kaplan, "Artificial Intelligence, Business, and Civilization: The Future Is Now." Journal of Business Strategy, vol. 41, no. 4, 2020, pp. 21-30 - Kaplan discusses the immediate and long-term impacts of AI on business and society. He emphasizes the need for strategic planning and ethical considerations in leveraging AI technologies for sustainable growth.

12. Andre Esteva et al., "A Guide to Deep Learning in Healthcare." Nature Medicine, vol. 25, 2019, pp. 24-29 - This paper provides an overview of how deep learning techniques are being applied in healthcare. It discusses the potential benefits for medical diagnosis and treatment, as well as the challenges in integrating AI into clinical practice.

13. Dario Amodei et al., "Concrete Problems in AI Safety." arXiv preprint arXiv: 1606.06565 (2016) - The authors identify specific technical problems that must be addressed to ensure the safety of AI systems. They propose research directions to mitigate risks associated with advanced AI, emphasizing the importance of robustness and reliability.

14. Yann LeCun, Yoshua Bengio, and Geoffrey Hinton, "Deep Learning." Nature vol. 521, 2015, pp. 436-444 - This landmark paper reviews the advancements in deep learning, a subset of machine learning that has driven recent breakthroughs in AI. The authors explain the principles of deep neural networks and their applications in various fields.

15. David Silver et al., "Mastering the Game of Go with Deep Neu-

ral Networks and Tree Search." Nature, vol. 529, 2016, pp. 484-489 - This paper describes how Google's AlphaGo program defeated a world champion Go player using deep learning and tree search techniques. It highlights the potential of AI to solve complex problems previously thought to be beyond its reach.

16. Ian Goodfellow et al., "Generative Adversarial Nets." Advances in Neural Information Processing Systems, 2014, pp. 2672-2680 - The authors introduce Generative Adversarial Networks (GANs), a novel approach to machine learning that involves training two neural networks to compete. GANs have since become a foundational technique in AI research.

17. François Chollet, Deep Learning with Python. Manning Publications, 2017 - Chollet, the creator of the Keras deep learning library, provides a practical guide to implementing deep learning models using Python. The book covers both the theory and application of deep learning, making it accessible to practitioners and researchers.

18. Melanie Mitchell, Artificial Intelligence: A Guide for Thinking Humans. Farrar, Straus and Giroux, 2019 - Mitchell offers a clear and engaging introduction to AI, explaining complex concepts in an accessible manner. She discusses the current capabilities and limitations of AI, as well as the prospects and ethical considerations.

19. Kate Crawford, Atlas of AI: Power, Politics, and the Planetary Costs of Artificial Intelligence. Yale University Press, 2021 - Crawford examines the broader societal impacts of AI, including issues of power, inequality, and environmental sustainability. She argues for a more critical and informed approach to AI development and deployment.

20. Anna Jobin, Marcello Ienca, and Effy Vayena, "The Global Landscape of AI Ethics Guidelines." *Nature Machine Intelligence, vol. 1, no. 9, 2019, pp. 389-399** - This paper surveys existing ethical guidelines for AI across different countries and organizations. The authors highlight common themes and differences, providing a comprehensive overview of the current state of AI ethics.

These expanded references will enrich your book by providing readers with a deeper understanding of AI and its multifaceted implications.

SELECTED BOOKS PUBLISHED
BY DR. SELVA

These books can be viewed/ bought by following the
link below to the Amazon site:

https://selvasmail.com/selvasbooks

Alternatively, should you wish to view the books on
your phone or tablet, you could scan the barcode below, which will also take you direct to the Amazon
site.

Scan me

BOOKS ON WELLNESS & HEALTH (7 BOOKS)

BOOKS ON ALZHEIMER'S DEMENTIA (6 BOOKS)

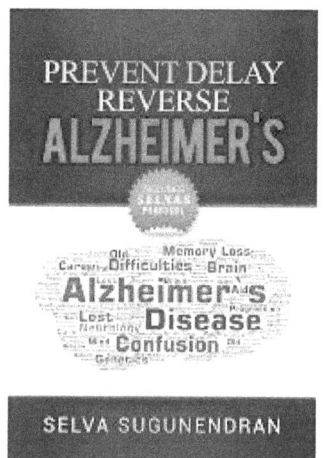

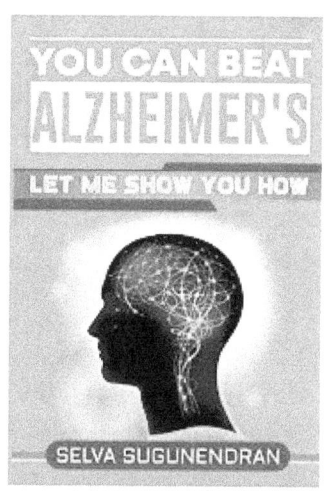

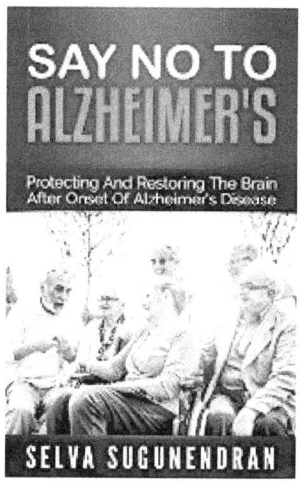

BOOKS ON SUCCESS (5 Books)

AI ROBOTICS (7 BOOKS)

CHRISTIAN BOOKS (18 BOOKS)

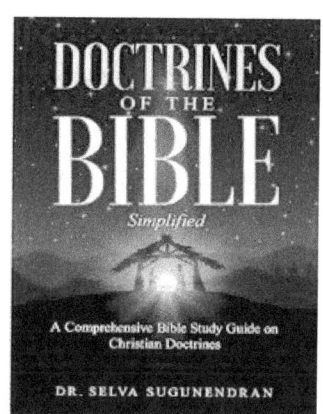

THE IMPORTANCE OF CHRISTIAN EDUCATION
FOR THE WELFARE OF CHILDREN

Christian Thought and Practice of Parenting and Educating Children About Church and God

DR SELVA SUGUNENDRAN

PRAYER IS POWERFUL

ORGANISED CHRISTIAN PRAYERS TO ASK GOD FOR HELP FOR YOURSELF & YOUR LOVED ONES

SELVA SUGUNENDRAN

PATHWAYS OF LIGHT:
WALKING THE CHRISTIAN JOURNEY

A comprehensive and accessible guide for newly converted Christians, helping them to navigate their new faith journey with confidence, support, and inspiration drawn directly from the Bible.

DR. SELVA SUGUNENDRAN

A LIVE DEBATE
AMONGST 3 YOUNG SCIENTISTS
On Eight Key Areas of Evolution

SELVA SUGUNENDRAN

21 REASONS
Why Evolution Lacks Scientific Proof

SELVA SUGUNENDRAN

BIG BANG
THEORY DEMYSTIFIED

SELVA SUGUNENDRAN

THE POWER OF DIVINE CONVERSATIONS
UNLOCKING THE SECRETS OF PRAYER

DR. SELVA SUGUNENDRAN

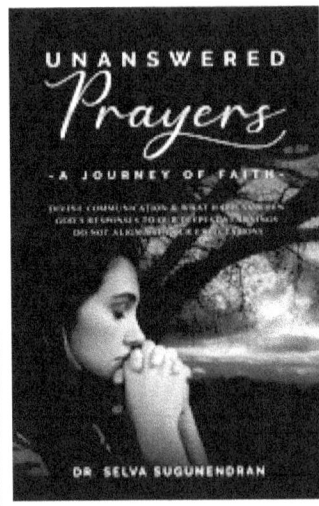

UNANSWERED Prayers
A JOURNEY OF FAITH

DR. SELVA SUGUNENDRAN

BELIEF BEYOND BOUNDARIES:
EMBRACING THE EXTRAORDINARY THROUGH CHRISTIAN FAITH

By
DR. SELVA SUGUNENDRAN

Appendices

1.   WEBSITE LINKS

https://AIRoboticsForGood.com

https://MyChristianLifestyle.org

https://BlessMeLord.com

https://HealMeLord.today

https://CreationEvolutionAndScience.com

https://AIRoboticsForGood.com

https://DementiaAdvice.care

https://HowToLeadAVibrantLifeWithAlzheimers.com

2. CONTACT LINKS:

The Author Email: Selva@MyChristianLifestyle.org

All Books by Author Available on Amazon:

https://selvasmail.com/selvasbooks